CONQUER
FROM WITHIN

6 Simple Steps to Unleash your Greatness and Elevate your Life

This book is a pre-launch copy. There are a few letters missing here and there. Hakuna Matata :)

by
Bruce Ellemo

To my parents Cecile and Norm, my step mother Anne, my brother Eric, my sister Tina and to Angela Gomez. I couldn't have gotten this far without all of your love and support.

To Ryan Oevermann and David Dines, your editing and input was invaluable.

TABLE OF CONTENTS

INTRODUCTION

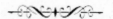

Life is an experience that is played out in our minds. Understanding our minds' inner workings and nuances is the key to finding health, happiness and joy for the time we are on Earth. Coming to terms with our mind is a monumental challenge we all face. If we are able to understand the machine that is our brain, we can truly enjoy life and all of its offerings.

We have all heard the saying "find yourself" or "get in touch with yourself" or in Shakespearean terms "know thyself". This is far more elusive and challenging than the words suggest. Getting in touch with self is hard because of all of the non-stop chatter in our minds. Constantly trying to make life act as to our likes and dislikes. Ever busy trying to create an environment consisting only of our personal preferences. Full of desires and forever chasing them.

Our minds run wild and without understanding what's happening the mind can become a runaway train. This is exactly what needs to be avoided. Be on guard against the wandering mind, the dominating mind, the confused mind. Letting the mind be in control can move us in the wrong direction, in the opposite direction and further away from that which we desire. The more we feverishly chase our preferences and desires is the less contact we have with true self.

Change your perceptions, change your life. The time of

enlightenment is here, it is time to find the peace of mind, that level of happiness that will manifest your greatness. Shake off the old and tap into your authentic self, find the hidden power, be a distribution centre of happiness, become the joy of a human that you deserve. Let's head on this journey together as we explore our souls and learn to understand who and why we are the way we are. Let's take the hidden path because it is one least taken. It is the path of all champions and warriors alike. It is in these pages for the taking, whether you implement it or not is completely up to you.

How do people create the strongest mind and soul? How does one repair, yes repair (a lot of people need repairing) a mind that has been hammered into submission by society, teachers, parents, friends, the media? How is a mind changed that has been shaped by every influential person around them since birth?

The solution is much simpler than you think. Many of our minds are preconditioned and preprogrammed from childhood and stick with us into adulthood. Many of our beliefs and perceptions are not ours but rather passed down to us from family and those around us. We just haven't put enough thought into it to try to determine why we have certain beliefs and perceptions or why we like some things and dislike others. You have been so busy creating the model or box around yourself that will keep you safe and secure when things get tough. You have been too busy creating the stories you tell yourself to insulate you when times get tough. You always have somewhere to hide and to retreat to when the outside world doesn't quite line up properly.

These models we build ourselves are only built with what we were taught growing up and what we have seen in our little world. You almost certainly have not built the proper model based on what you know and have seen to date. There is so much stuff that you haven't seen, don't know and aren't privy to. Your model has probably already been tested in life because that's what life does, it throws tests at us. How did your current model stand up to the divorce, the death, the betrayal or the deception? Did it get knocked down just like you did? There is a better model for us that we didn't know about. Let's work through this model in these pages. It is my sincere desire that in these pages you find the unstoppable power that is contained in all of us.

I am not sure what happened along the way, whether it is lack of gratitude, human complacency or just a sense of entitlement but we have forgotten how much of a true miracle we are just being a human being. We all came to be from something we can't even see with the human eye, we came from virtually nothing. And here we are roaming the Earth with eyes, lungs, a body with a mind that has thoughts and emotions. On top of that these bodies are self- healing. We have been given the ultimate machine in the form of our bodies and our minds. What we do with it is up to us.

We will examine and design a state of being with an inner world that is substantial, powerful, at peace and fl wing. Throughout this book we look deeply at developing and fin - ing your authentic self, the one behind the mask. It won't be hard work, you will find this to be easy and without effort. It is an effortless process to be and find yourself. All we need to do it sit back behind our thoughts and objectively look at ourselves, as if we were another person listening to our thoughts. We are not our thoughts, we are the consciousness behind our thoughts. We are the "self" or the "soul" that either intentionally or not, conjures up the thoughts. Differentiating the two is critical for balance and existing in the middle ground.

I have written this book to provide a mirror into yourself. My intention is to provide a reflection of yourself to yourself. Because in the end aren't we all the same? Contextually we all want the same things, just the content differs. The fundamentals of being a human are the same, we are all truly the same. Throughout our journey you will be able to take a valuable look inside your mind and you will become pleasantly surprised at how much you are already very intimate with, while it may not feel like it.

In these pages we shall go on a journey to contentment and fulfillme t. Your insecurities, fear, lack of empowerment and blaming will slowly disappear. As you work your way through this book you will become intimate with the inner power to conjure up energies of strength at will. You already know how to find yourself, you just got disoriented and distracted along the way. Retuning and redefining yourself has never been more important than right now. We can either live our lives from memory or from inspiration. You want to come from inspiration.

How people treat you and how you perceive the treatment by them is a big part of becoming disoriented in life. We shall develop the ability to secure and nurture strong relationships. You will learn to release your blockages, shred your insecurities and build the wonderfully strong and happy human being that you are supposed to be.

Disappearing will be the constant need to analyze and evaluate everyone and everything. The brain wants everything to be right all the time, you will learn how to be OK with everything in life, just the way it is. We shall walk the tightrope of the middle ground together. Once you realize that it is ok for life to "go wrong", your mind will stop evaluating and trying to fix everything, relieving you of great stress and anxiety. You will be able to take a seat in "yourself" and let life be what it is. You will no longer struggle with the relentless inner voice that can hijack you at any time, that voice that conjures up misguided thoughts, the voice that is self-sabotaging and self-defeating. What we shall do together is change your perception of your life. We are going to let "you" take the driver's seat.

Once you are able to get in behind your thoughts and sit in the seat of "yourself" you will become at one with the world and the people in it. Your mind will quiet and the incessant chatter will slowly fade away. Your job isn't to understand why you have all the thoughts or fight with them. Never fight with your mind, you will never win. Just sit back and objectively listen to all of the thoughts that you have. Let them fl w through you, do not act on them as if they are designed to guide you. Your soul is the one that guides you through this life. Have you ever heard the term, we are in borrowed bodies and simply passing through? The soul is the one in charge, not your mind.

Learn to relax in behind your thoughts and just notice them, allow a new perspective to unfold, one that is quieter, less judgemental and amazingly free. A mind free of noise has no option other than to bestow peace and happiness. A quite mind is an open heart, an open heart is an open soul and an open soul, by its very nature, defaults to love and peace. All you need to acquire life's abundances, is a soul and the desire. These are both free and in all of us. And should you choose to devote yourself to the ongoing journey of self-realization you will develop unbelievable mental strength and power.

When our minds are right and our souls are free, we can begin the journey of unlocking the authenticity and power within, bringing your authentic self to the surface for all to see. Together, we shall look to unearth the warrior inside, allowing your primal best to surface. We all possess a magical spirit that wants to reveal itself. It is time to take the mask off, take a deep look inside and become the original that you are. Taking yourself to the Promised Land of authenticity will be the finest journey you will ever go on. You will become bridled with confidenc , inner strength, peace and happiness with energy that will move people and yourself, beyond measure. You will secure a happiness and joy you could have never have imagined.

We shall take this new found energy and apply it to daily habits making you unstoppable. You will begin to look inside yourself and see what is required to operate at your best level both on the inside and out. You will learn how to live with power and grace as the eagle flie . It is my sincere hope that you will become the best version of yourself, live a great life and enjoy peace within.

CHAPTER 1

WEIGHT OF THE WORLD

Your inner essence and magic is not another's, it is your own. It does not require deep studies or hard, arduous journeys to attain it. It is the innermost essence of ourselves. Common sense thinking as to how anything comes to be anything will soon convince us that our great inexhaustible life must be the very root and substance of every fibre of our being. Take advantage of this power within. Once released, your entire existence will shift into another gear. You will immediately feel a rise in excitement and possibility.

Life rarely unfolds exactly the way we want it to, which makes a lot of sense. The earth has been around for a few billion years, we will be here for one hundred years if we are lucky. The events that are transpiring in front of us are truly miraculous and are the culmination of universal forces that have been occurring for billions of years. The fact that we are not in control of life's events should be evident to all. We are not responsible for most of the events that transpire in our lives. Yet, we walk around trying to control all that has happened, is happening and will happen.

It is no wonder why people are filled with tension, anxiety and stress. We all seem to believe that life should be as we want it; as opposed to allowing it to be a natural result of universal fl w and natures forces. Without knowing it, we do this with most things in our lives: we actually believe life should work out according to our likes and dislikes, exactly how we want it. This way of living poses huge challenges, it begins to create a perception that everything has to be the way you want it all the time and when life is not how you like it, there must be something very wrong.

Every day we give precedence to our minds thoughts over what is actually happening. We will say things daily like "it better be warm today because I'm going golfing" or "she better say yes to that date because I really like her," or "I better get that raise because I really need the money." Notice how these meaningful claims about what should and shouldn't be happening are solely based on your personal preferences and have no grounding in scientific evidence? It is through this mentality that we feel that the world around us is supposed to manifest in accordance to our own likes and dislikes. This can lead us to feel like we are always struggling with something in life.

We can begin to believe that life is a struggle because it is not working out the way our minds believe it should. When life doesn't work out the way we think it should, we create a resistance to people and events because surely it can't be my fault? We start to believe that the world is working against us and we resist accordingly. I would prefer it to be the way I like it!! Why isn't it going the way I want it to? This is also known as carrying the weight of the world on your shoulders. We are either pushing or pulling energies away from us or towards us, without really knowing what is truly good for us. This battle between individual will and the reality of life unfolding in front of us can end up consuming our lives. If we want to understand this experience within us, we must look at why we think life should be a certain way. In a lot of cases, we don't even know why we want things a certain way, we just do. Let's take a step back and look a little deeper into ourselves for the answers.

Society, our teachers, our friends, our parents, the media and the world at large has taught us our values, our perceptions and our metrics of life. That someone will win and someone will lose, that someone is right and someone is wrong. We have been taught what to value and how to value it. We have been taught how to think and what to think about. From an early age we have been pigeonholed into these codes of conduct, behaviours and beliefs.

Whatever you have done up to this point is just a duplication, a reproduction of what you believe subconsciously that you deserve and what is possible for your life. Most people operate out of their personal history, out of their memory, things they have done, things they have experienced, things they have seen, things they have observed. What I am suggesting is that you operate out of a larger vision of yourself. I want you to see yourself doing what you want to do, experience what you want to experience, have what you want to have, doing what it is that gives your life some meaning and value. Operate out of your imagination, not your memory.

This is easier said than done as the persuasiveness of these influen es are exceedingly powerful. You are constantly being reminded of what you should and shouldn't believe, and what all the family members have always believed, and what will happen to you if you ignore these beliefs. Fear becomes a constant companion of your beliefs, and despite the doubts you may have inside, you often adopt these beliefs and make them crutches in your life, while you hobble through your days looking for a way out of the traps that have been carefully set by generations of believers before you.

"The persuasiveness of these influences are exceedingly powerful"

Growing up, the only references we have as to how we should behave is through our friends, our parents, our teachers, the media and society at large. This is where we develop our perceptions, attitudes, behavioural patterns and general outlook on life. These formative years are the groundwork that establish a lot of who we are. If you are not happy with some of the ways you think, speak, behave, act, etc., recognize where they came from and, more importantly, start working on removing the characteristics you don't like. It really is that simple to create yourself. If you yell at your spouse, there is an extremely good chance that your father yelled at your mother and I'll bet that his father yelled at your grandmother. Stuff just gets passed down from generation to generation, that's just the way it is, good, bad or indifferent, like it or not. Creating your own "self" the way you want to be is part of the growth process.

Realizing that you have this ability to keep only the characteristics you like and discard the rest is part of maturity and is a must on your way to enlightenment. You don't want to yell anymore, acknowledge why you react this way, someone implanted it in you growing up, and simply tell yourself that you are no longer a yeller because you don't like it, and it's over. It is not necessary that we continue the way we have been taught or shown or know. There is absolutely no reason why anyone should have to model themselves after their parents or their friends or society if it was less than stellar.

How we were raised becomes hardwired into us as the rules that should govern our life and also as a loose basis of how other people should run their lives. We believe that we shall have our best opportunity at a full life if we abide and stick closely to the rules that were taught to us through society, parenting, friends, etc. These "rules" become the foundation on which we build our life and perceive the world. We come to believe that anything different or in opposition to "our rules" or "beliefs" is wrong or strange in some way. Our "life rules" become so entrenched in us that, if someone behaves in contradiction to our rules or thoughts, we can have a diffic lt time accepting that person's behaviour or position in life.

We all were raised in totally different environments with different parents, different friends, different outlooks and completely different experiences, so it makes sense that everyone thinks and behaves differently. Just because behaviours and actions are different from the way you behave, speak and act doesn't mean it is wrong. The way you behave and act is only right because you think it is right. Other people may think your behaviour is odd and peculiar. They are right as well because it is what they believe is right.

There is nothing more important to personal development than realizing you are not the voice of the mind but rather you are the one who listens to it. If you become willing to objectively observe your thoughts, you will soon see that most of them have no pertinence. They have zero effect on anything in your life, they only affect you and how you feel and the decisions you make based on them. Thoughts make you feel better or worse about what is happening in your life, what has happened in the past and what will happen in the future. The day will come where you will understand how useless this involvement can be and how it is not life causing the problems but your overactive mind really causing all the problems.

"There is nothing more important to personal development than realizing you are not the voice of the mind but rather you are the one who listens to it."

Day in and day out, we walk the earth evaluating people and situations, casting judgement on whatever or whoever comes our way. Why do we evaluate, judge and form opinions around people and events when we see them? While we often form wonderful opinions about people, there is a default switch in our minds that hijacks us and says to us, "that guy looks dodgy" or "he should back off the hot dogs" or "she looks strange" or "that hair is ridiculous" or "he looks poor or rich" or a million other things we say to ourselves? *Judging people is a massive burden to our overall happiness and well-being.* Through judging we separate, through understanding we grow.

Try to suspend your judgements of those who are less ambitious, less peaceful and less loving and instead know that hatred and judgement are the problems in the first place. When you judge the haters and hate the judgers, you are part of the cancer rather than the treatment.

What would happen if our minds perceived nothing to be wrong and everything and everyone is exactly the way it/they should be? Think about that for a moment; what would it be like to have a quiet mind? This is where magnificent radiance comes from, this is the epicentre of confidence and the wellspring of happiness, a quiet mind is the hallowed ground of peace. A quiet mind is a powerful mind.

**"The ability to observe without evaluation is the highest form of intelligence".
- J Krishna Amrit**

Carrying the weight of the world on your shoulders is no way to live and is a saying that has been around for many years. This, of course, is a metaphor meaning that your mind is foggy, not clear and is brimming with negative thoughts, stress and anxiety. If your mind was clear from the incessant chatter, it would have nothing to think about except that which gives it purpose and fulfillment. You would be free to create, grow, manifest and truly fulfill your purpose. Instead the opposite can occur where we live in opposition to people and events. We allow our mind's thoughts to distract us away from what we know we need to do to enjoy all of our desires. We give our time, attention and energy to thoughts that are completely useless, unnecessary and odd at best.

Think instead about how to grow, how to make life better, how to change, how to better serve, how to create a better tomorrow. Do not waste your time and energy on fabricating, creating and being a slave to useless thoughts that never come to see the light of day. This is not the way of a warrior, this is the way of the weakened and frail. When we give our thoughts and energy to the right things only, we create a ripple effect that will be your guide to your best self. You are freeing up your energy to allow other energies from other people and the universe to enter. You begin to allow positive energies into your psyche that come from non-resistance. The same event you resisted before can become an opportunity if treated with non-resistance. When you are blocked, guarded, angry, over thinking, trepidatious and afraid. There is no room for the good energies to fl w in; they get blocked at the gate.

Happiness is when what you think, what you say and what you do are the same. - Gandhi

7

When you live from this happy place, you are living from your heart and when you live from your heart, there is no gravity. You don't feel the weight of the world on your shoulders. Your so called insurmountable problems disappear and instead of your problems you get possibilities. The mind will run wild if you don't reel it in. What happens when we let our minds get into overdrive is we are thinking exactly the opposite of how we really want to. What we end up doing is asserting our will in opposition to the fl w of life.

Resistance and blockages are always the result of an event or occurrence that happened in the past. The event has already happened, why resist it further, why create an energy around it that moves into your psyche, through your mind and into your body and soul? All for what, so you can be unhappy and shut down? We are distancing ourselves from the state of happiness whereby what we think, say and do are the same. We want to relax our minds and slow down so we can sleep but we can't sleep because the mind is running out of control and it won't let you sleep. I'll bet you have even tried to yell at yourself to shut up. Then you realized that you're yelling at yourself and that won't work.

"Resistance and blockages are always the result of an event or occurrence that happened in the past"

The mind has a powerful way to think about an event that happened and replay it as if it is happening again in the present moment. At times the mind is unable to differentiate whether an event is happening in real time or happened in the past. You can think about a loved one that died years ago and start cry-ing. The event is over but the thoughts of the death make you cry even 10 years later as if the event is happening now. You can think about the time when you stubbed your toe and a few minutes after can still recall the pain. You can think about great sex you had and your body can twitch and quiver 20 minutes after it's over, as if it is happening now.

The mind is a powerful thing and it must be understood. You are the only one that can do this and it is mission critical. When you lie in bed at night and let your mind run wild, you are torturing yourself. Stop this. You are repeating the undesirable event over and over in your mind as if it were still happening. The main reason people can't sleep is they can't shut down their minds. I have spoken with many people who have described these pre-sleep hours as torture. Always remember we are all the same, we are all simply in pursuit of happiness, love, purpose and peace of mind. Put your problems in perspective, we are all just human beings spinning around on a planet in the middle of space pursuing happiness, love, purpose, peace of mind and some material things. Once you realize this and take it to heart, you will begin to see people in a new light. You will say to yourself, "he or she is just like me", because they are. We are all trying to do the same things.

This perspective will allow you to not be judgemental of anyone or any situation. Everyone is simply trying the best with what they have been given. Why we judge people or situations or talk negatively about people is rooted in self-fear, anxiety and personal insecurities. Anxiety is simply the fear of the unknown coupled with a feeling of hopelessness. If you're both fearful and harbour feelings of hopelessness, you will have anxiety or be stressed out. The word anxiety is interchangeable with the word stress. People have anxiety or stress because they become out of balance. What they think and say and actually do are not in synchronicity any more. This is where we think one thing and do another. Someone may design a great plan to lose the weight but have found themselves slamming back a bag of potato chips and some chocolate bars. Johnny told himself he was going to stop drinking but is fi e beers deep and just getting started.

"Lying to ourselves is by far the most impactfully negative thing we can do"

Thinking and wanting one thing but acting in opposition to those thoughts can become frustrating and demoralizing. After enough of these inner energy tug of wars the innermost oppositions begin to manifest into its physical counterpart as anxiety and stress. This is why you see people who are stressed out and full of anxiety speaking of life not going "their way" and that "nothing is right". Well that's because nothing is going right, including, and most importantly, the relationship they have with themselves. They are lying to themselves, they are not living in reality. Lying to another person, as lying to yourself, carries massive consequences. Lying to ourselves is by far the most impactfully negative thing we can do. It is always best to be honest with yourself. Personal honesty guarantees a bridge between the mental gaps of what you want versus what you are doing. Being honest with yourself takes a great deal of pressure off of your mind. If the gap is too big between where you are, what you are doing and where you want to go, you will constantly find yourself unable to reach your goals. If this is the case you can either **downgrade your desires** to match your effort or **increase your effort** to match your desires. Either one of these approaches will get you closer to your goals. The human brain has an amazing ability to reconcile this cognitive dissonance.

When we take the position that life just is what it is and no one is right and no one is wrong, when we take the mindset that each situation is not right or wrong and just is what it is, we reset our minds to a fl wing mindset. We have let go of ourselves. A fl wing mind is crucial and the foundation of a wonderful and happy life. There is really no reason for anxiety or problems. Tension and anxiety only happen when you resist life's events. If you are neither pushing life away, nor pulling it towards you, then you are not creating any resistance. You are simply present and in the moment, where the magic lies. This is the preferable state where you are simply witnessing and experiencing the events that are taking place in your life. If you can commit to doing this you will see that life can be lived in a state of peace. Move freely around the earth, unencumbered by thoughts about where you *should* be and how you *should* be acting and what you *should* be saying. Listen to your inner callings, ignore how others might want to direct your life energies, and allow yourself to radiate outward what you feel so deeply inside you.

"A flowing mind is crucial and the foundation of a wonderful and happy life"

As you explore internally the first thing you will realize is that most of your mental activity is focused around your likes and dislikes. If you have a preference towards something, you will think about it and talk about it. If you dislike something, you will carry it around with you and speak about it, giving it life. It is these mental preferences that will create all the ongoing dialogue about how to control everything in your life. We are very accustomed to manipulating our thoughts so that we feel that we are in control. You need to be very careful with this. When the voice narrates the outside world to you, now those thoughts are side by side with all of your other thoughts. All of your thoughts begin to intermix and influence the experience of the world around you. What you end up experiencing is personal narrative of the world according to you, rather than the unfiltered experience o what is really out there.

When you decide to stop listening to all of your preferences and dislikes and instead start the willful practice of accepting what the fl w of life presents, your mind will be quiet. You will marvel in a quiet mind, one that is accepting, one that is curious to another possibility and one that begins to desire life in different ways. If you truly begin to examine your preferences, you will soon see that you aren't even sure why you prefer certain things, you just prefer them. Once you examine your preferences and why you prefer them, it will help to change your perspective on them, perhaps taking you in a different direction in life.

When life or an event doesn't perform to our likes and preferences, we resist the event causing a negative energy to build inside us with every resistance. Over time this changes the core of your being through molecular manipulation. Resistance causes a negative trigger of the mind causing the atoms in our bodies to change and these mind/body changes manifest into its physical counterpart as anxiety and stress. If we want to understand this tendency, we must first understand the reason why we are so resistant to life. If you look inside yourself you will soon see that it is you, you are the resistance. You, the person who is behind all of the thoughts, you are your soul, you have the power.

They have a name for this and it's WILLPOWER. It is the fabric of everything we do, going to bed, waking up, working, procreating and even thinking takes willpower. Being alive is willpower. We all have it, the question is, how much willpower are you using in your life to create your best life? Our willpowers must be tested and sharpened all the time. Once you have been able to harness your will power, it can be used to great effect.

"If you look inside yourself you will soon see that it is you, you are the resistance"

Let's look at why we resist life sometimes. Bad things happen to good people, this is life for us all. We all know what it feels like when something bad or negative happens to us. It has a powerful effect on our minds and spirts. Bad things take a tremendous toll on us. It is what it is, bad things hurt. Here comes the problem with having bad things happen. These become blockages and in turn become disturbed energy that sits in your body and mind. What happens when we have negative situations in our life is that we allow the problems into our hearts, we let these situations seep into our spirits and take root in our souls.

If you let enough of these disturbances stick in your body, you will be very unhappy, unfulfilled, sluggish and perhaps depressed. **You must not let the blockages stay in your mind and your soul, you must release them**. Practice taking inventory on your thoughts. Begin with the little things. For example, you are walking down the street and you see a person that you think you know so you give them the head nod and they don't nod back. You are not sure if they didn't see you or if they don't like you or whatever is making your mind race a mile a minute. Good time to relax and take some inventory. It's all good, everything is ok, no need to think about it all day or sometimes even into the next day. If they did see you and ignored you, who cares? There are eight billion people on the planet; get over it.

Disturbances begin with getting pulled down into the disturbed energy with an event in life. If you resist a life event that unfolds in front of you causing you to build some negative energy around it, you end up exactly where you don't want to be. The last place your consciousness needs to be is down there, but this is where it gets pulled to. Now when you look at life through your disturbed energy, everything is distorted through the haze of your disturbance. Things that looked beautiful once now look dark and not so beautiful. Things you once liked now are not exciting or even depressing. But nothing has really changed. It is just that you are looking at them through the eyes of disturbance.

You must leave this seat of disturbance as quickly as you can otherwise it will affect your relationships, your business, your success and happiness in life. The disturbance or blockage will manifest itself in everything you do, your thoughts, words and actions. You will now look at life through this darkened fi ter. When the blockage manifests itself, you are passing it on. When you dump your stuff into the world, you are creating your world and existence.

We all know that what we put into the world is what we get back. What you will find if you let these disturbances manifest is your whole world will be filled with exactly what the disturbance is. The blockage is always something that happened in the past. This is how people ruin themselves and relationships. Their blockage becomes triggered and they start to behave as if they are in the moment that blockage occurred, all of the event's emotions are released into the world again but now towards yourself or your partner. No partner, either personally or business related, will tolerate this baggage over time.

Watch your thoughts as you watch the street traffi . People come and go; you register without response. It may not be easy in the beginning, but with some practice you will find that your mind can function on many levels at the same time, and you can be aware of them all. It is only when you have a vested interest in any particular event that you gets caught in it and you black out on the other levels. Even then the thinking on the blacked out levels goes on, beyond your field of consciousness.

Do not struggle with your memories and thoughts; try only to include in your field of attention the other more important questions like, why am I here? Who am I? How did I happen to be born? What is this universe around me? What is real and what is momentary? What is my purpose?

You are always seeking pleasure, avoiding pain, always after happiness and peace. You must see that it is the very search for happiness that makes you feel miserable? Understand that *you are* happiness and there is no need to look anywhere. Try the other way: indifferent to pain and pleasure, neither asking nor refusing. Give all of your attention to the level on which "I am" is timelessly present. Soon you will realize that peace and happiness are in your very nature and it is only seeking them through particular channels that disturbs.

To seek there is no need, you don't need to seek what you already have. You are the supreme reality. Eventually you will become wise enough to not want all this stuff inside you regardless of what or who stimulates it. Enlightenment is the ability to feel the energy build up in you and say to yourself, "It doesn't matter if I think this is right or wrong or fair or unfair or even makes sense, I'm just going to leave it alone and let it be." This wisdom will afford you an enormous amount of time to be used more constructively. To laugh, to exercise, to stay still, to be quiet, to speak to someone uplifting, to help another out. The amount of mental energy and free time you will receive from avoiding these negative channels will be your reward.

"It's not that the mind has to be quiet; *you* have to be quiet"

Sometimes you will catch yourself in a heightened state of the racing mind, slow it down and don't get involved with all the thoughts, let them fl w through you and don't allow them to touch your core being. If you keep an eye on these daily thoughts, you will soon see that you can let them go as easily as they came in. You will soon be able to realize that these thoughts serve no purpose and are just passing thoughts that hold no meaning. It's not that the mind has to be quiet; *you* have to be quiet. Choose to act on only the thoughts that in some way make you feel inspired or put a smile on your face. Under no circumstances are wild or misguided thoughts to be acted on. If the thought isn't inspiring, doesn't fit into your core principles or causes you to take a step backwards let it pass through.

We are so in tune with ourselves that we have an ability to feel our thoughts. You know, the thoughts that make your spine shiver or body shake, the thoughts that put goose bumps on your arm or that smile on your face? These are the thoughts we need to pay special attention to and act on when realized. The thoughts that inspire you to act, the ones that make you feel good, the ones that give you joy and offer happiness. These are the types of thoughts that we must act on and act fast with vigor. This is being authentic to yourself, **this is the very first step to authenticity.** The ability to let the meaningless, purposeless and otherwise useless thoughts pass through us and pursue only thoughts that come from love and joy and happiness is the noblest of endeavours and is at the core of happiness and authenticity.

After we absorb and internalize only the inspiring thoughts our energy changes for the positive, the vibration on which you operate increases in frequency. This is where the world will begin to listen to the nature of your song. This is where the right people are, this is where the right opportunities are, this where you should be and will be if not there already.

If you really want to grow inside, you must let go of all of your preconceptions and stuff. Growing is recognizing that all of your stuff is what is keeping you trapped. Once you have been able to release your stuff you will soon see that life has actually been trying to help you all along. Life is never against anyone. People are against themselves and they only feel like the world is against them. When you hear people complain about how the world is out to get them, just realize that it is them who is getting them, and no one else. The universe doesn't want to get anyone, it just wants to act the only way it knows how. Life is filled with inspiration, growth, opportunities, love and only wants to provide you with your desires, but it must act in accordance with its own natural laws, NOT YOURS. Nature is only interested in forcing everything to act in accordance with its laws.

"The universe doesn't want to get anyone, it just wants to act the only way it knows how"

You have been in your own way the whole time and you didn't know it. You have been unable to see that your resistances have been the problem. You have not been able to see that carrying around your stuff has been why your shoulders are heavy with the weight of the world. You have given your mind the impossible job of making sure everything is right all the time and exactly the way you want it. True personal growth is going beyond the part of you that is not all right and requires protection. This is achieved by always remembering that you are the one inside objectively listening to the voice talking. **This is the way out.** This is the path to the core of your being, this is your soul. If used properly, that same voice that has been the epicentre of all your problems, worry, stress and anxiety, it can become the launching ground for spiritual enlightenment. Once you are clear that you are the one observing the voice, you will have come to understand one of history's greatest secrets.

To begin with, trust me. It enables you to take the first step and then your trust will be justified by your own experience. In every walk of life initial trust is essential; without it little can be done. Every undertaking is an act of faith. By remembering what I said; you will achieve everything. I am telling you again, you are the all-pervading, all-transcending reality. Behave accordingly; think feel and act in harmony with the whole and the actual experience. You are pure greatness. Exactly the same greatness that creates all of life. Keep this thought first in your mind and you will attract to yourself the same powers of creation. Greatness attracts more if its own self to itself the same way that thoughts of lacking act upon a belief that ensures the lacking becomes your reality.

How do we release the blockage from the past? You let it go. Is this easier said than done? NO. You just don't let it in. Yes, it is that easy. When the event happens and it doesn't feel good, you know that it is a disturbance. Consciously tell yourself not to think about it and do not give it ANY energy. It is our choice to give energy to what we choose. Be very careful what you give your energy to. Energy is your power, so do not give it away to occurrences or happenings in life. Protect your energy!

Clint Eastwood, movie actor and director, was asked at age 88 (in 2018) what keeps him going? Where does he get the energy from? His answer: "Every morning when I get up and look in the mirror, I say to myself, "don't let the old man in"" and he doesn't. Clint is still making movies, playing golf, working out, doing public speaking engagements and making T.V. appearances. He refuses to give energy to something that will drag him down.

Let's look at another of the pieces of life that has a massive impact on whether life is viewed as a struggle or a magical experience: desire. Desire is simply craving the memory of pleasure. Desire is defined as a strong feeling of wanting to have something or wishing for something to happen. Desire, at its core, is the want to repeat an act that made you feel pleasured in the past. If we didn't have memories, then we would simply be in the present moment without distraction. We would not remember what brought us pleasure and therefore would have no need to chase down pleasure all the time. We would be in a state of active, open, intentional attention on the present, otherwise known as "being in the moment". When we are "in the moment" or are present in our timelessness, we are truly alive. Monks live this way, where there is no pleasure and no pain. They seek nothingness making them "in the moment."

Which is probably why there are very few monks, this mindset doesn't work for most of us. We don't have the time to sit on the mountaintop for years burrowing down into the tiniest cracks of our minds. Most of us are working diligently day to day, grinding, striving, and accomplishing things. The challenge with our way of life is that in order to satisfy our desires for pleasure we need to work hard and keep up the pace. In order to keep up the pace and gather what your mind desires you need discipline.

Developing discipline is tough. Being disciplined by managing your urges is required to live your best life. We have urges for almost everything in life, good, bad and in between. Urges are defined as impulses to engage in a habitual behaviour or past addiction in physical sensations in the body, not just in thoughts. Think of urges like ocean waves, whereby they rise in intensity, peak and then eventually crash. We must surf these urges and act only on those that inspire and ignite us, letting go of the rest. We have been gifted the ability of self-control, it must be activated to achieve greater heights.

"Urge surfing can be thought of as an exercise for training your self-discipline and mental toughness. It is meant to teach you how to embrace discomfort and resist temptation. Our natural tendency is to identify with our urges and urge surfing helps us to separate our identity from whatever past habits and tendencies we want to correct. Instead of thinking, I want a smoke, you might think, I have an urge to have a smoke. It is not a part of you that you must fight, but rather a sensation that you experience, observe, and the let pass or settle.

"Urge surfing can be thought of as an exercise for training your self-discipline and mental toughness"

Fighting urges is rarely effective, but curiously observing urges without identifying with them gives you much greater odds to overcome them. The power of the urges comes from your willingness to indulge in them, not from the temptations themselves. Another useful metaphor for this internal struggle is to think of urges as a waterfall, where battling the urges is equivalent to trying to block the waterfall... Of course, it is inevitable that the waterfall will break through, perhaps even more forcefully than it originally was because the pressure built up trying to block it. Mindfulness is the escape from this impossible scenario because rather than trying to block the waterfall or urge, you step away from it and just watch it. This strategy is crucial to identify, as implementing it is one of the most effective ways to improve self-efficac .

If you can successfully change your attitude about urges and temptations to one of curiosity instead of fear or resignation, you'll also be able to change your behaviour. If you resist your urges you are setting yourself up for failure. In learning to accept and observe them, you make it possible to watch them quickly fade away. We are only interested in effective and sustainable solutions. In the case of overcoming urges, that solution is surfing the urge. In learning to be disciplined, you become comfortable with the discomfort of seeing an urge and not indulging in it. It is far more comfortable to judge our urges and to view them as the enemy, but this mindset will always acknowledge the urges we want to eradicate. Start taking an interest in your urges and studying them or experimenting with them, you'll learn that you are not the urges you feel until you succumb to them. As long as you simply observe them coming and going, they lose much of their power to negatively influence our behaviour.

Thought patterns are established by the repetition of the same thought. Thought patterns are established because of inherent or acquired desires or motives. That is, habits begin as the result of definite desire. Desires are organized impulses of energy called thoughts. Desire is a powerful force on its own but once emotion creeps in, you now have a very powerful seductive cocktail. If you become hijacked with emotional desire in the form of a triggered disturbance, anything thought prior to this is taken over and these emotions create the dominating thoughts which are always acted upon first

"Thought patterns are established because of inherent or acquired desires or motives"

Be on guard for disorganized thought patterns because once this action completes in the mind, it will quickly manifest into its physical counterpart, which is whatever has disturbed you. That is to say that once the disturbance is activated, you will behave and emote as you did during the original event, you will relive the event over and over. You are essentially torturing yourself. Be vigilant about your thought patterns and what you think about on a regular basis. What you think about creates your vibrational state and your vibrational state of being becomes who you are.

You don't need to join a monastery or sit on a mountain top for years to be in the moment or have a good vibrational state. It does take some work though. There are some things that must happen. You must leave your past behind you, your past is only a story in your head now, and it's just a memory. No memory will persist if you lose interest in it. **It is the emotional link that perpetuates the bondage.**

There is no need for your past to control your today, there is no need for the weakest part of your life to run your life. Yes, I understand that some pasts are more difficult than others but the fact remains, it's over, in the past and only a story in your mind. Giving energy to our past serves as one of the largest blockages or disturbances found in humans. People carrying these disturbances around for months and even years. When these blockages are triggered by current events, we head straight back into the disturbance as if it is happening in the current day. It is mission critical to remove these disturbances from your soul. How is this done? When you feel the trigger occur, recognize it as such, surf it for a minute and let it crash. Then simply give it no attention, energy, or thought.

"There is no need for your past to control your today, there is no need for the weakest part of your life to run your life"

Yes it is that simple. You control to what you give your energy and thoughts and this is a big one. Will is a real force that resides inside you; it is what makes us operate every day. Don't think you don't control your will and that life just kind of happens. We do the things in life that we give our will to. The power of self, when concentrated and funnelled into the mental, physical and emotional realm, creates a force we call Will. You have the power to affect things; do not think for a minute you are helpless in there.

Past disturbances and blockages must get no attention otherwise they will remain in your soul forever affecting your life. Once you have managed to give it no energy, it will slowly disappear and you will wonder why it was even a blockage in the first place. Blockages from the past cause much disruption in your current life. They affect relationships with others, your spiritual growth, your work, and your potential. Blockages have and can dominate people's lives to the highest levels; blockages are dangerous.

The other requirement you need be in the moment, is to not be afraid of the future or the unknown. Don't be a slave to what you don't have and what you don't know. It is not our job to know when, how, why and with whom it's going to happen. We don't have a crystal ball, no one does, so why spend time and your valuable energy on what might hap? I am not saying don't plan your future and think about how you would like things to be. Visualization is a tremendous tool for humans to realize outcomes before they happen. Just realize that it will never turn out or be exactly as you want it to be. This is the reality we all live with. Once you are able to realize this, we are able to be more flexible in how it turns out. Enjoy not knowing how it will turn out, enjoy the unknown, and do not be afraid of it.

The effect that we can have on the future is much less than what we believe it to be. This is where a lot of frustration and anxiety comes from. We want the future to look a certain way and are determined to ensure it turns out that way. We will do whatever we can to fight for the future that we foresee in our minds. The problem is that the future rarely if ever turns out the way we want it to. Once we take a back seat and accept the fact that we don't know how the future will turn out, a calm will prevail over you.

"Your ONLY job is to maintain your daily habits and disciplines that work towards your goals and to not stop until you WIN"

Your job is to put forth the best effort every day and allow the ripple effect to take place. Allow the interest to compound as a metaphor. Our daily discipline and perseverance is like throwing a rock into the water and seeing the water ripple. Every little victory that we accomplish stacks on top of the last victory and has an impact in your life that you haven't realized yet. Now you will see that it is not up to you to know the future, it is not your job to know how it will all unfold. It's impossible for you to know so let it go and say to yourself, "I have no idea how this will turn out but I am excited to see how it does unfold and I welcome all of the adversity and challenge along the way."

A fl wing mind doesn't let everything get stuck in your soul. Let's face it, we all get hammered with a fair bit of shit in life, a fair bit of negativity reaches us all. It is our choice what we let into our hearts and souls and what we give energy to. **Herein lies the key to happiness and flow: Only allow in what you choose to allow in.** You are the creator of your life, no one else gets to do this job for you. It is incumbent on you to create the best life possible and the best self. Don't give your energy to people and situations that don't deserve your energy. While I will never understand it, I believe the reason why we give so much energy to negative people and situations is because that is all we have known. Negativity is what we heard growing up, this is what we hear on TV, this is what our friends tell us, negativity is prevalent in our society. The TV will spend 55 minutes of an hour broadcasting all the negative things happening in the world and they will spend 5 minutes on a feel-good story of the local community person who lifts people up; bizarre but true.

Close your eyes for a minute while trying to stop your thoughts. This is the purpose behind meditation, to slow down the mind. How did it go? Were you able to stop your thoughts or did the incessant chatter jump in? This illustrates that you are not your thoughts? What were you thinking about? They are just thoughts and most of them don't matter. This is why it is important to separate who you are, your consciousness, from your thoughts. When you start to explore consciousness instead of form, you realize that your awareness is limited and small because you are focusing on small and limited objects or ideas. When you pull back into your consciousness the world will be less of a problem.

You are not your thoughts, your thoughts are simply thoughts. You are the person behind the thoughts or you are your conscience. Do not let your life be run by your thoughts. Instead, let it be run by your conscious self. To help understand this better, let's look at your mind. If you were to let everyone in to your mind so they could hear and listen to all of your thoughts, do you think anyone would want to hang out with you? Probably not. Some of the things we think of as humans are unnecessary, wasteful, strange and not productive at all. This is why they remain thoughts and not actions.

The incessant chatter that goes on in your mind can be dominating and affect your life. You are not your thoughts. You are the consciousness or soul sitting inside and behind the thoughts. When you sit inside yourself objectively and listen to the incessant chatter, most of which will never materialize, it is easy to see you are not your thoughts. Most thoughts have no significance or importance. A lot of our thoughts turn out to be a complete waste of time and energy. Once you begin to sit back and objectively listen to yourself, you will begin to be able to sift through the thoughts; the ones that count and the ones that don't matter at all. In fact, once you take the seat of self, the incessant chatter will slow down if not diminish entirely and you will find yourself only being inspired by thoughts of joy and peaceful thinking.

Once you are able to separate yourself from your thoughts and, in addition, realize that there is no right and wrong way of behaving as described earlier in the chapter, this massive weight will lift off your shoulders and you are well on your way to peace and happiness. Once you can shed preconception and settle into the understanding that no person is right nor another person wrong, you immediately free the space of your mind like additional RAM does on a computer. Imagine what it would be like if you didn't have to think all these useless thoughts all day. Think about all of the positive thoughts that you could allow into your head. Imagine if you didn't have to analyze and evaluate every situation and person. Take a minute and think about your life if you just accepted everything just the way it is.

You can have a different relationship with your mind, free from worry, free from stress. It can be where every day is a holiday, where you love exactly where you are in life from the minute you wake up until you go to bed at night. Remember, from the beginning, you have given your mind the impossible task to make everything right. You have told it to do everything it can to make sure the future turns out to be exactly as you want it and that today is exactly as you wish. You have told your mind to make sure your parents are satisfied with your life, you have had to satisfy an unregulated ego and make decisions based on societal and peer pressure.

You have told it that when it sees something it doesn't believe is right, to make it right. The problem is, once it has balanced out the current injustice, the next perceived injustice is just around the corner, it will never stop. Simply relieve your mind of this job, the job of making sure that everyone and everything will be the way you need them to be so that you can feel better inside.

TAKEAWAYS

- Let things be the way they are without your interference. Resistances to life's events cause stress. It is OK for things to be the way they are.

- Your thoughts, words and actions must align with your desires.

- Feel your thoughts. Act on thoughts that inspire you. Allow the meaningless thoughts to pass straight through you giving them no meaning or emotional attachment.

- The universe doesn't align itself to your likes and dislikes. It has a fl w that you must become part of, not the other way around.

- The more you resist that worse it is. Resistances, through molecular manipulation, turn into psyche changes. Psyche changes are not what we want.

- There is no need to judge or analyze every event for meaning.

- Do not get pulled down into the disturbances. You cannot let the weakest part of your life run your life. It is only when you have a vested interest in any particular event that your attention gets caught in it.

- Be very cautious as to what you give your energy. Energy is your lifeblood, so do not give it away to occurrences or happenings in life. Protect your energy!

- The universe does not tolerate idleness, complacency or vacuums of any sort. All space must be filled with somethin

- Only allow into your life what you choose to allow in. If you don't like it don't let it in. Only give your energy to that which serves you.

CHAPTER 2
BARRIERS TO HAPPINESS – THE POWER OF BEING FREE

Happiness is transient by nature; happy one minute and not so happy the next. Wouldn't it be great if we were happy all the time? We will never know because that type of ability isn't available to us and may not even be good for us in the end, we'll just never know. What we do know is that we want to be happy as much as we can and as often as we can. It is the most favourable and sought after state of being. The only emotion that beats happiness is love. Love is what creates happiness. The answer to being happy is quite simple. It is the understanding of your resistance to your perceptions of life; the understanding of your inner energies and how they can become disturbed through your resistances and blockages.

To have happiness means we are content and fulfilled. It's just another choice we have to make. What do I want for dinner, what do I want to do tonight, what are we going to do this summer, do I want to be happy regardless of what happens. Am I unconditionally committed to being happy? If you are not ready to make this fundamental decision you will most certainly not get to where you want to go. Happiness is not found at the finish line. There isn't even a finish line. Life is not a race to be finished; it's a dance to be danced. And only if we allow ourselves to enjoy the dance, can we let happiness in.

One day your life will flash before your eyes and you don't want to see all of the irrelevant and unnecessary things roll by. Life is happening right now. We've got one shot, taste the thrill of life. Remember that energy, in whatever form, must go somewhere and become something. Be very careful with your energy. It can either lift you to the space of greatness or take you down into an abyss of mediocrity. Happiness knows only multiplication, accumulation and increase. Unhappiness knows only sorrow, despair and melancholy. This could be one of the last chances you get so make this one decision to be happy regardless of what happens, then sit back and watch the world change around you. Too many of us believe that happiness is a future event. Before we arrive, we need more money first, have a successful career, find a partner or settle down. Only then will we arrive at the destination of happiness. But when we arrive, we will realize happiness isn't there. Happiness is in your mind, you create it. Happiness is self-created. Unhappiness is also self-created.

Happiness means everything is in order, including the mind. The mind has found rest and reprieve when all is in order. One of the mind's purposes is to try to make everything ok, to make sure that anything that may be slightly off balance is repositioned in proper order. When something gets "out of order", the mind jumps right in and starts to try to make it all ok and balanced again. When people try to make their outside world match their likes and dislikes they become unhappy as they are not living in reality. Life doesn't act according to people's likes and dislikes.

You need to reconsider this single perception as it may change the direction of your life. It has never been that way for anyone and will never be. We have all encountered things we didn't want or ask for; disease, death, car accidents, broken bones, deceit, lies, and the list goes on and on. It is just how it goes; this is being human and being alive. You need to become ok with the fact that everything isn't exactly as you want it. Also remember that, in a lot of cases, the way we want it isn't always best for us. We just think it is best for us based on our perceptions. A lot of the time we chase our desires around only to find out that that wasn't really what we wanted, we just thought we wanted that. To be happy is to let go of outside circumstances, turn inside work on yourself, and let life chase you not the other way around.

When you start to let go and let life be the way it is without your interference, your resistance to events in your life will taper off. You will begin to let your guard down and your mind will ease. When life doesn't go your way you will be ok with this because you expected it to go that way. This is how life is for all of us, it always doesn't go our way. We all have problems, it is the way we respond to them that really matters.

"When you don't involve yourself in all of life's little events you free yourself of the minutia of life and begin to focus on the big picture"

When you look at life this way, you begin to free up your biggest resource, your energy. No longer will you go down into the valley or spend your time on meaningless people or events. Events in your life will become not worthy of you giving up your energy and time. When you're not involving yourself with all of life's little events you are elevating yourself. You are freeing up time to be used for growing yourself and achieving your goals. When you don't involve yourself in all of life's little events you free yourself of the minutia of life and begin to focus on the big picture. Don't spend your time wallowing in other people's minutia either. Humans are notorious for having small problems that they love to drag other people into.

When you let go, your "difficulties" will be treated exactly as your "wins" are, easily and without effort. When you let your guard down to life, you will expect life to not go the way you want it. You will see that life isn't always about things going right. If you live in reality you know that life doesn't always go the way we want it. Be ok with life not going exactly the way you want it.

When things don't go the way we want them there is an automatic resistance to what is happening. The resistance occurs when the brain perceives that things are not ok. When the brain thinks things are not ok, it begins to push or pull the event towards or away. It begins to attach emotion to the event. These perceptions then cause the mind to want to say something or do something about the event to somehow influence it. As a result people jump into conversations and situations that they shouldn't. You then begin to involve yourself with other people's business. This is the first barrier to happiness; over-involvement.

Over-involvement

There is huge tendency to over-involve ourselves in life's minor events, to want to step in and let people know how we feel, to project one's will into an event to try to affect or shape its outcome. There is no better example of over-involvement than in children's sports. Parents berating each other, screaming at the referees; it is terrible behavior. Who in their right mind screams at a 14 yr. old referee because of a call that perhaps wasn't the correct one? Even worse, who in their right mind starts yelling at the other parents during a game they aren't even playing. We see over-involvement on social media, in business, in relationships, with our children, amongst friends, in politics and above all in our own minds.

"There is huge tendency to over-involve ourselves in life's minor events"

Over-involvement has a direct effect on the levels of our happiness. There are so many things we don't know in life but for some reason we have to make life and the events in it exactly as we think they should be. If you really must involve yourself, involve yourself in situations of good, charity, kindness, giving back and acts of love. These involvements will lift your spirit and strengthen your soul.

An over-involvement scenario may look like this, "I can't believe that guy called my friend an idiot at the office today. I'm going to talk to him next time I see him and sort this out". In this case, the mind doesn't see balance, it sees mistreatment and in its perception this behavior is wrong and must be somehow fixed. The mind's job is to perceive that everything is squared up, level and correct. The mind wants everything to be the way it thinks it should be. These are your perceptions of life. Your mind has built up your model of what life is and when events don't fit into your model, surely they must be wrong.

There is no right or wrong in this situation and almost all others we encounter. Maybe his friend is an idiot. They are adults, if they don't like being called an idiot they can handle it. Maybe those people were smirking at John, taunting him, which is why he called them idiots. There are a lot of reasons why someone calls someone else an idiot but in this case it is none of your business. Yes, there are some injustices and mistreatments that need to be dealt with accordingly, it is the other 99% this book is concerned with.

If we can change the perception of how we view the events as they unfold in our lives, we can keep in closer touch to happiness; perception is everything! When you involve yourself in other people's business, well, you are now in other people's business, often knowing nothing truly about it. Let's start by taking care of our own business first. Once you have mastered yourself, people will begin to ask you for your thoughts and opinions on different issues, you won't have to jump in and over-involve yourself where you don't belong. Until that time, stay away from offering unsolicited advice or imposing your will into situations and events that are not yours. Let it be the way it is, it's ok.

"The only true wisdom is in knowing you know nothing" – Socrates

When we spend our energy on these perceived imbalances of life, we aren't giving ourselves the time or leaving ourselves the energy to concentrate on being content, happy, purposeful, creative, moving forward and not standing still. People create problems where there are none; we manufacture problems. Problems create backward movement that have heavy consequences that take a toll on their lives and those in it. We may not feel it at the time because we are busy "making everything right" but the truth is over-involvement is being out of control, in other people's business, attracting negativity, lowering standards and in the end letting yourself down. Our over-involvement merely serves to give us more things to think and talk about and gives us further permission to not focus on the most important thing which is you. The mind has a wonderful way of creating thoughts that distract you from your goals and dreams.

"People create problems where there are none; we manufacture problems"

How many times have you been lying in bed going through the all the possible scenarios of how a situation unfolded or may unfold and ended up awake for hours and hours ruminating, hypothecating and wildly fabricating outcomes. It is no wonder people have such difficulty sleeping, their minds never rest, constant internal drama and creation of non-sensical thoughts. As much as you believe you will "solve" the situation or "set the person right" or "fix the event", it rarely if ever does, so do yourself and everyone a favor, leave it alone and let it be the way it is.

Let people go through their life experiences and allow them the freedom to deal with it on their own; this is where great lessons are learned. If you are constantly imposing your will and opinion on other people, not only are you degrading your own happiness but you aren't letting other people grow and figure out answers on their own. People need to have their own experiences, not hear about yours. Once you take the position that there is no need for your unsolicited advice, you free up a lot of time and energy to focus on events that make your heart sing and give you the most happiness.

> *"To enjoy good health, to bring true happiness to one's family, to bring peace to all, one must first discipline and control one's own mind. If a man can control his mind he can find the way to Enlightenment, and all wisdom and virtue will naturally come to him". Buddha*

It is incumbent on all of us to take care of our well-being and happiness. This is only a job that can be accomplished first in your mind. It can't be overestimated or overstated how important it is to be careful what thoughts you allow to seep into your psyche and soul. When a negative, destructive, self-sabotaging, non-loving or otherwise useless thought comes into your brain, let it flow through you and do not attach any emotion or further thought to it. If the negative thought is about what someone is thinking about you, stop it in its tracks because they aren't thinking about you. If the useless thought is that you can't do something, disregard it and go the other way with it; you know it can be done. You know all the ludicrous stuff you think about. Put an elastic band around your wrist and every time you think something negative give it a good snap and snap yourself back to reality. Don't think about it anymore. Yes it's that easy.

This has been the whole problem the entire time. You have been letting all your thoughts go past the gatekeeper, your soul. The life event is occurring and you are placing a resistance to the event, giving it life. This is why you are so busy inside your mind because you haven't been the gatekeeper of your thoughts. You have allowed them to flow in freely without allowing the soul to process the ones that need attention. You have been giving way too much emotional attachment to your thoughts. They have been pouring in by the millions and you have given your mind the impossible job of sorting through them all and making sense of everything. You have been letting all your thoughts just pour in and take hold. Once you're enlightened, you will understand the absolute ease at which these thoughts can just pass right through you, keeping you in the moment, where you belong.

If you want to try to understand why you resist some life events and not others you must look at the value or the meaning of the emotion you have attached to the event which disturbs you. It is not the event that is disturbing, it is the emotion you are having as a result of the event that disturbs you. It doesn't feel good so you resist. Do not resist the event, simply allow the emotion you are having to settle and disappear. You have to surf these waves of thought that control our emotions, letting some of them crash down on shore disappearing from your mind. The root of these associated emotions will almost always be found in your childhood and your upbringing. Something happened along the way that disturbed you greatly and that is why you resist certain events and not others.

It is important to take inventory here. The question you must ask yourself is: Why I am always feeling this way about this type of event? Why am I resisting? Why do I consider life to be a certain way? Why do I value the things I value the way I value them? How am I choosing to measure myself? By what standard am I judging myself and everyone around me? These values you will find are often not values you created but values that were handed down to you through your upbringing, society, friends and your untrained unconditioned mind. You must reframe the event in your mind attaching different value, meaning and emotion to it allowing the event to more easily move through you, without disturbance. Simply put, if your response to an event is causing you stress or anxiety you are looking at it the wrong way. If you were looking at it the right way you would be in balance with yourself and there would be no stress or resistance within. **Once you understand and implement this simple act of thought you can change your entire life forever.** You must do the work to look inside for the reason or the cause of your resistance and emotional attachment to events. This is the way out.

Whether we like it or not, we are always taking an active role of what is occurring to us and within us. We are always interpreting the meaning of every moment and every occurrence. We are always choosing the values by which we live and the metrics by which we measure everything that happens to us. Often the same event can be good or bad, depending on the metric, the value or the emotion we choose to give it. In other words, how do we perceive life?

"It is critical to look inside to understand why we value things in life the way we do"

Value and emotion underlie everything we are and do. It is critical to look inside to understand why we value things in life the way we do. Why? Because everything we do, think and say, day-to- day is based on why you value what you value.

What if you are choosing a poor metric or standard for yourself and your life? Is it possible that you have looked at life's events wrong? Is it possible that your values have been handed down by someone who didn't have the greatest values? What else could be true that you are not considering? What is objectively true about your situation is not as important as how you choose to see the situation, how you choose to value it and what emotions you place around it. Problems will always be around, what is most important is the meaning you place on them. We get to control what our problems mean to us based on how we choose to think about them and the standard by which we choose to measure them. The great enemy of the truth is very often not the lie (deliberate, contrived and dishonest) but the perception (persistent, persuasive and unrealistic).

We must challenge why we think about life the way we do. We must acknowledge that our values, viewpoints and perceptions can be and often are wrong. Uncertainty removes the judgement we have on ourselves and others. Uncertainty is the root of all progress and all personal growth. The man who believes he knows everything learns nothing. The more we admit we do not know, the bigger the opportunity to learn. Before we can change our values into better healthier ones we must become uncertain about our current values. We must mindfully strip them away, exposing their weaknesses and biases and recognize how they don't fit in with the rest of the world.

"Uncertainty is the root of all progress and all personal growth"

Some of our values are faulty and incomplete, and to believe they are perfect is to put us in a dangerous mindset that produces entitlement and avoids accountability. Let's take a look at how distorted values and perceptions of life cause us our greatest problems. People can emotionally swing from being happy and having tremendous well-being, to being in a "valley" a "slump" or a "rut". There are highs and lows in life, that's just how it is and has been from the beginning of time. Almost all of these "valleys" or "lows" are self-created. Yes there are things out of our control: the economy, natural disasters, what other people think, death, etc. This book focuses on the things we *can* control, our perception, our response, our emotions and our work ethic.

It is clear without question that the difficulty people find themselves in are of their own making. More than that, their difficulties are seldom the outgrowth of immediate circumstances. They are generally a culmination of a series of circumstances that have been consolidated through untrained habits and thoughts. It takes a lot of time to break down and get in a valley, it slowly consumes you.

"Problems and difficulties are generally a culmination of a series of circumstances that have been consolidated through untrained habits and thoughts"

Constant and steady neglect over time is the life flow of the valley. Negative emotional attachment to life's events is the bloodline to the valley of the lost soul. Once the mind starts to perceive something as a problem, it can shut us down physically and mentally. It can start to take over and consume you from the inside out. The mind will steal all of your energy and in some cases take over and run your life. Having difficult times in life or being in one of life's valleys is a rite of passage for all people. The valley is where we all go through to gather our wisdom, hindsight and battle scars. Valleys are the learning ground of champions and the enlightened. The big question is, "Why do we have to go there so many times, when we know better?"

Become intimate with the process below as it will give you the necessary insight to stop the "valley" or "rut" from happening, saving you all sorts of time and grief. What we want to do is understand the process and realize what is happening and when it is happening. We want to acknowledge when it is happening and stop it before it gathers life, we want to stop it in its tracks. The degradation process is the same for all of us. Don't think you are alone or on your own when you reach the valley floor. This valley floor is well worn by all people, regardless of race or ethnicity. And if you are like most of us you've surfed life's valley floor on more than one occasion.

There is no need to engage the valley any more. You no longer need to spend any of your precious time wasting away in the valleys of life. Once you understand the process you will know how to stay out of the valley, keeping you vibrant, alive and in the moment. So much time is wasted in the valley. Why would we allow ourselves to go into the valley? The answer is because we didn't know how to avoid it. No one told us what was happening. Life was just happening and we had to deal with it without knowing anything about it. There we were, lonely, sad, little or no money, lost our job, unhealthy, got divorced, was cheated on, deceived; whatever it was, we had to deal with it without knowing how. No one gets a roadmap of life. We have to experience the valleys to understand how to stay out of them.

"Understanding how to avoid the valleys or low points we encounter will save you time, energy and your resources"

Wise people feel the disturbance hitting them; they acknowledge its presence and immediately transfer all energy away from it until it is gone. If you have these disturbances inside they will always be getting hit with something in life, you can't run from them. Someone or some event will always manage to bump into your disturbance bringing all the emotions to the surface. By immediately diverting this emotionally charged energy upon being triggered, you are controlling the energies you allow into your mind and body. Using this technique you will be able to avoid the valleys or low points in your life. The **Degradation Process** chart below outlines the complex process of how we get into the valleys or low points of our lives with little or relative ease.

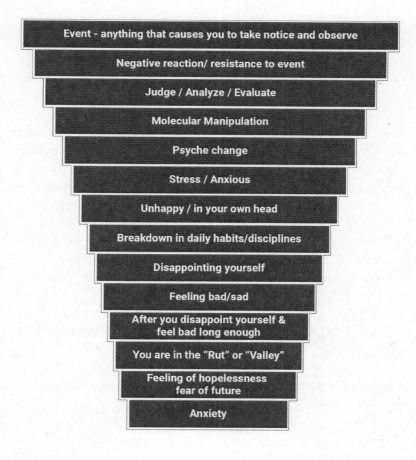

Event - anything that causes you to take notice and observe

Negative reaction/ resistance to event

Judge / Analyze / Evaluate

Molecular Manipulation

Psyche change

Stress / Anxious

Unhappy / in your own head

Breakdown in daily habits/disciplines

Disappointing yourself

Feeling bad/sad

After you disappoint yourself & feel bad long enough

You are in the "Rut" or "Valley"

Feeling of hopelessness fear of future

Anxiety

The valley is the place where you feel weakened, anxious, stressed, fearful, lonely, and sometimes desperate. All of us who end up in the valley get there with the same mental process. Understanding how to avoid the valleys or low points we encounter will save you time, energy and your resources. When you stay out of the valleys or extremes you will be preserving your time and energy for lofty endeavors. Staying out of the valleys is what wise people are very good at.

Let's explore the process. Once you have seen an event happen that doesn't fit into your life model or that you perceive as right, wrong, unjust, intolerable or however you perceive the event, it has now gathered your attention only if for this brief moment. What happens next is you will then analyze, judge and evaluate to see if it fits into your world.

The events that you cling to and label as "need my attention" are the ones that you've given emotion to, it means something to you. You have a value or emotion attached to the occurrence, you may know what it is or you may not, it doesn't really doesn't matter. This is where you start pushing, resisting the event with your mind, your energy and your thoughts. It is here where the cerebral snowball begins to roll. If you are able to stop the mental spiral here, it is best to do so because from here, it starts to seep into your soul, which we want to avoid.

DON'T HAVE NEGATIVE RESISTANCE TO EVENTS

Let them be the way they are. You don't always have to understand everything.

Now that the event has entered your energy field and mind

immediately, and without knowing it, a molecular manipulation occurs within you; a molecular manipulation in your mind that has been brought about by the energy of your thoughts. Your negative thoughts that are resisting the event have disturbed your psyche by placing a negative emotional attachment to it.

Once the psyche is disturbed, the disturbance slowly finds its home in your heart because this is the center of our energy. Everything goes to the heart including all disturbances, resistances or blockages. We need to protect our heart as to what we allow in it.

After your resistance to the event has entered into your heart, its resting place eventually is in the soul. Once you have allowed it into your soul, you are fully enveloped in the struggle and are fully disturbed. Once you are disturbed, it only gets worse. This is merely the beginning of the needless mental battles you are about to fight. If you can stop the process here, it is very well advised to do so or it will just get worse.

Now the blockage has entered into you and you are fully engaged. You are waking up with it, going to the bathroom with it, thinking about it all day, taking it for a walk and going to bed with it. This is like another piece of clothing, engulfing you, always on. You talk about it, think about it, use it as an excuse, tell others about it and live your life through its lens. This is about the time where the stress and anxiety start to creep into this downward spiral. You are spending so much time thinking about the disturbance. It now has the life within you that you have given it. Now that you are anxious, stress fractures will begin to occur. Your mind will create stress, think stress and seek stress from here on out. Stress is the typical path that negative disturbances take. We all know what stress feels like. It can and will take over us if we let it.

Happiness is the next thing to go. Remember, at this point

in the process, you are choosing to move further away from the goal which is happiness. If you are feeling the stress or signs of shortened temper, heightened emotions, anxiety and a short fuse, you must recognize that the disturbance has entered and you need to simply let it pass through. It is never too late to just say goodbye to the blockage as it attempts to crowbar its way in or has taken root. Allowing it to remain inside will only allow it to gather momentum while it plots the next attack. Not only are you overly suspicious thinking about the problem all day but you have allowed it to steal your one ally; happiness.

"Daily disciplines and constructive habits are the very first things to start to weaken and disappear as you allow the disturbance to consume you"

Without happiness and with the blockage burrowed in deep, you are in the choke hold of the valley. You are nearing the half-way point to the bottom of the valley of the lost soul. I am hopeful you are able to see how all of this started. It started with the initial resistance to an event. The good thing is you can still take this time to stop your descent. If you can reframe your perception of the event giving it less emotional attachment, you will stop the blockage fl w and in turn, your downward spiral.

If you can't stop it now then you're on the tipping point. If you can't reframe the perception, unhappiness will do what it does best and knock you to your knees. Now that you are there, its physical counterpart of behavioral breakdown is right around the corner waiting to run with the baton. Daily disciplines and constructive habits are the very first things to start to weaken and disappear as you allow the disturbance to consume you. When your perceived "problem" happens, the mind jumps in and hijacks you, telling you that "there is no way I can keep up my daily disciplines, I am hurt and in pain". It is as though the mind says to you, "I have to suffer, this is terrible and the only solution is suffering".

We then begin to attach more and more emotions to the "problem". Once this dangerous emotional cocktail we are now drinking has had enough time to take over the mind and body we begin to completely stop doing what we know we should be doing. When we perceive emotional pain, it's almost like the mind has a shut-off switch that permits weakness to enter and overcome all who encounter it. Don't misunderstand me; it is important to heal and emote and go through what you are going through but try to keep perspective around the event in check as best you can.

If your boyfriend, girlfriend or spouse left you, so what? What's wrong with the wrong people leaving your life? You clearly aren't supposed to be with them. They may actually be doing you a favour and saving your time and energy. You should be thanking them not suffering and torturing yourself for months or years on end. Why would you want to be with someone who doesn't want to be with you? Let it go; there are 8 billion people on the earth; move on.

When a low phase enters into our lives the first thing we give up are our daily habits. Our daily habits become victim to the emotions we associate with the "problem" or the "perceived pain" and we begin to stop doing the exact things we *know we should be doing.* For example, we know we should be eating properly, sleeping well, exercising, reading, educating ourselves, going out into nature, getting up early, being kind, generous, loving, working hard, loving, being disciplined and contributing to society. When life is firing on all cylinders this is the formula we all use.

"Depending on how big you perceive the problem to be is how much time you will spend with it"

What happens when the mind goes into the thinking mode of, "We've got a problem", it is the same as how blood immediately rushes to a physical injury on our bodies. A physical injury will create an immediate reaction of the body to push more blood to the wound. This is the body's way of trying to heal itself. The same can be said for the mind when it perceives a problem. The mind reacts by pushing all thoughts and energy toward the problem; it draws all of your mental resources. Depending on how big you perceive the problem to be is how much time you will spend with it. Sometimes the disturbance can invade for only minutes, other times days, even months and in many cases years.

When we allow our minds to get hijacked by our problems, our energy shifts towards them and we can become lethargic, lack purpose, be angry, be sad, be lazy, be afraid and, in a lot of cases, depressed. Our perceived problems are the culprit and they commence the hijacking process in our minds, which in turn maneuvers and manifests into its physical counterpart through the breakdown of our daily habits, choices and disciplines.

It becomes increasingly difficult to focus on the plan we designed for ourselves because the disturbance is taking up too much of your time and energy. It's what we think about all the time whether consciously or not; it sits on us like the weight of the world. All of a sudden, we don't jump out of bed at 5am anymore, we sleep in. Bedtime goes from 9pm to midnight, those two glasses of wine turn into a bottle and our smile disappears from our face. Very quickly our diets begin to erode followed by negative self-talk and all of a sudden bam. You're in the valley. Yes, the same one you have been in before, perhaps many times. Wouldn't it be easier if you just avoided this place? There is a reason the bible says that we "Walk through the valley of death". It says this because we walk *through it*. It does not say to set up camp and live in the valley of death. The point is, difficulty and struggle come to us all in many forms. It is not that it comes, it is how we deal with it.

Internal disappointment stemming from poor choices leads to further degradation of behavioral patterns and drives you further into the valley. There is good news however, internal disappointment is the major precursor and precipitator of human change. Once people have disappointed themselves long enough, they change. It can take days or it can take years, but after a while, almost everyone has had enough. Let's take the degradation process to the end.

The degradation process carries on. Now that the daily disciplines and habits are out the window, the hollow feeling of internal disappointment starts to limber up for its imminent playing time. When we stop executing our daily habits long enough, we begin to disappoint ourselves because, along the way, we knew what we were doing. We knew we were breaking our daily habits and disciplines. When we stop doing the things that we know we should be doing, quite naturally we know we are not doing them.

You have said to yourself before, "I should stop doing this" but kept doing it. We've all told ourselves that we will do something and haven't done it. This is disappointing to you, whether consciously or not. Lying to yourself can be very disappointing, leading to that inner feeling of a dark empty caressing anger. Once you have danced with empty anger long enough, you have officially entered the alley of the lost soul.

The valley of the lost soul or the "perceived low point" in someone's life is the home of sadness, despair, lethargy, helplessness, anxiety, lack of purpose and stress. No one wants to be here but it is a human right of passage; we all must pass through the valleys of life. **What is way more important than passing through is knowing how to stay out of the valley in the first place; that is wisdom.** We are going to learn how but it is important that we take the process to the end for the sake of understanding.

The thoughts we think and the inner dialog that we engage in most every minute of every day has the greatest bearing on our health and well-being. Once our minds break down, our bodies soon follow and weaken. The thinking patterns that you have, the way that you emote internally about yourself and others will have the greatest bearing on the vitality of your body. The reason is because internal thoughts create chemical changes in the body, each and every second.

A person who lives in happiness and appreciation with a positive, optimistic outlook on life, despite its challenges, will enjoy a stronger and healthier body than someone who is negative, dark, and pessimistic. Even the simplest of words that we use with ourselves and with one another mean so much as they can evoke a positive or negative chemical change instantly in our bodies. For example, a simple compliment given to a co-worker, "You look very nice today, Judith", can positively change both of your chemistries for several hours. It feels good to give, and receive! Unfortunately, the opposite is also true: "I look fat in these pants" will negatively impact your body and will reinforce the negative aspect(s) you really want to change.

Instead, think and act positively, and, if something is not the way you want it to be, then take the necessary action to improve or correct it. If you're a human, this is just the deal: the mind is always working, thinking and looking for something to do. If our brains weren't wired this way, then we wouldn't have electricity, planes, iPhones, and may still be sleeping in caves. *This growth, creativity and vigor of the mind is your most valuable asset that needs to be harnessed for its fullest capacity to be realized.*

The reason you are in "another slump" is all because you stopped doing the things that you know you should be doing. Once we have hijacked ourselves with our "perceived problem" and we have entered the valley or low point in our lives, it can spiral downward quickly if something isn't done to remove the disturbance immediately. If the disturbance isn't removed, we begin to disappoint ourselves over and over by making decisions that we know we shouldn't. These poor decisions reflect directly on our daily habits whether we execute them or not. Speaking poorly of others, not exercising, complaining, overeating, staying up too late, sleeping too much, watching too much TV, being nonproductive, lacking discipline, no self-control, being antisocial and lazy to name a few of many.

"You can't fuel a Lamborghini with leaded gasoline"

The problem with adapting invasive qualities like these is that they are contrary to how we are designed; they go against everything humans are designed to be. We are designed at a DNA level to be productive, to get ahead, to progress, to grow, to design, to create, to love, to act. Our brains are wired for constant activity: we have 60-80,000 thoughts a day; brains never stop even when we are asleep; it is what it is, recognize it. Our bodies are also designed to handle this massive cognitive function up to the point where our minds break down. Allowing these invasive qualities into your mind is the quickest way for your mind to break down. Your mind is searching for peace, order, happiness, joy, gratitude and love and you are feeding it with complaining, lethargy, lack of discipline, negativity, poor thinking and lies. You can't fuel a Lamborghini with leaded gasoline.

It is absolutely possible to go through your life with no problems. It is only a problem if you perceive it to be a problem. A different perspective can and will completely change the direction of your life. "Where are the problems?" Ask yourself. Is your internal dialogue telling you that your problem is loneliness, not enough money, not enough love, too fat, too skinny, unhappy at my job, lacking purpose, car sucks, not enough adventure? Whatever you are telling yourself is exactly what you need to start making a plan for. These are your desires, not problems, listen to them and act on them. These are "problems" for everyone, you are not special in this regard. Everyone gets lonely, doesn't have enough money, is lied to, gets fir d. Some people simply exert enough of their will-power and discipline to make sure they solve their "problems".

"It is only a problem if you perceive it to be a problem"

Other people seem to think these "problems" should be solved for them just because they are on Earth. Some people allow these so called "problems" to completely take over their lives and steer them into the ditch. Let's just acknowledge that we all have these problems and we are simply trying to design a plan to shore it all up, to make it exactly as we want it. We are all trying to design our ideal life. Anything worthwhile and lasting takes a couple of years of hard work and patience. Design a two year plan around what you desire.

If losing twenty pounds and having a svelte body is what you want, your plan will involve creating a good meal plan and carving out exercise time at least 5 days a week for an hour. Do that for two years, being disciplined and consistent, and I guarantee that you will be a new person, with increased vitality, strength and outlook on life. Imagine if you did this for 4 years, even 10 years. Very few things worthwhile in this life are immediate. Building something worthwhile takes minimally 2 years and more often a lot longer than that. To go from being lonely, sad and isolated to being a social butterfly will most certainly take years but if that is what you want GO DO IT. Make your plan and get after it but be prepared, it won't be easy, you'll want to quit. DON'T QUIT, and always remember why you started. You will get there with your new found patience and understanding of the process. One to two years creates something ok, two to fi e years creates something worth talking about and fi e to ten years builds greatness and legacy. You must be patient. A farmer doesn't dig up his seed to check on it, he waters it with faith.

"You must not design your life around protecting yourself from your insecurities. Go on the offence"

Let's say your internal dialogue is telling you that you are lonely and sad. To work your way out of your perceived problem here, you need to make a plan centering on time for yourself, being social, working on your relationship skills and elevating the frequency you are on. If needed, there are professionals in your area that specialize in being social. Why not pay a visit or two with a professional to get some tips and ideas on your social plan? After that, it is time to jump in and start getting out to the establishments where people hang out. Don't take yourself too seriously, no one else does. Like any plan that yields results, you need to be consistent. Your new social plan may include going to the pool once a week, joining a sporting group or co-ed team or going to a bar/eatery once a week, maybe hitting the nightlife on the weekend, perhaps a beach in the sunshine. I guarantee you that if you work your social plan consistently for two years you will no longer be lonely. You must get out and attack your insecurities or blockages, you must not design your life around protecting yourself from your insecurities. Go on the offence, it will change your life forever. You will love who you become. Can you think of any reason you wouldn't want to be in a great relationship, be fit, healthy, wealthy, happy, full of love and full of contentment?

Let's say your internal dialogue is telling you that you don't have enough money. If this is the case, the plan you make needs to be around earning more money. There are literally thousands of ideas here but build your plan for two years out and be ready to work that plan. Lean into the daily habits that you designed to make the money you want. Find out what you love to do, whether it is selling things, making things, writing things; find whatever it is and do that. If you need money right now, go get a job, work for someone else until you have saved enough money to start making money with your passion. Everyone has to pay the bills, getting a job working for someone else will provide you the immediate cash fl w required. It is after hours where you chase your passions; you build and execute your two year plan. "That seems like a lot of work" you may be thinking. It depends on how hungry you are. Chasing down your dreams and having your desires fulfilled should provide enough motivation to get you going.

The Past

The *number one* reason people struggle with happiness is that they carry their past around with them like a life sentence, giving it energy day after day, year after year and believe it or not, sometimes a lifetime. People have past disturbances that remain with them in their current day that have not been dealt with and released. A lot of people are unable to get out of their minds and souls the blockages or disturbances of the past. The divorce, the breakup, the job loss, the law suit, the death, the business failure, the betrayal. A lot of bad things happen to good people, it's how we perceive them and how we release them that really matters. Haunting yourself with your past difficulties and disturbances does no good for anyone, most importantly you. There is no benefit to you, in fact, the only thing you get is grief through mental and physical suffering. The stress that builds up kills people. Worrying about something from the past is like praying for something you don't want to have happen and praying for it every day.

Forgiveness of self and others is the key to removing the disturbances. Disturbances range in intensity but almost always another person is involved. When you forgive yourself and then forgive the other person, you will begin to heal the mental laceration. Forgiveness is the intentional and voluntary process by which a person undergoes a change in feelings and attitude regarding an offense, and let's go of negative emotions such as vengefulness, anger, hostility, and even hatred. Who hasn't been hurt by the actions or words of another? Perhaps being bullied, a colleague sabotaged a project or your partner had an affair or simply people deceiving you. Or maybe you've had a traumatic experience, such as being physically or emotionally abused by someone close to you.

"When you forgive yourself and then forgive the other person, you will begin to heal the mental laceration"

These wounds can leave you with lasting feelings of anger and bitterness. But if you don't practice forgiveness, you might be the one who pays most dearly. By embracing forgiveness, you can also embrace peace, hope, gratitude and joy. Consider how forgiveness can lead you down the path of physical, emotional and spiritual well-being. Forgiveness means different things to different people. Generally, however, it involves a decision to let go of resentment and thoughts of revenge. The act that hurt or offended you might always be with you, but forgiveness can lessen its grip on you and help free you from the control of the person who harmed you. Forgiveness can even lead to feelings of understanding, empathy and compassion for the one who hurt you. Forgiveness doesn't mean forgetting or excusing the harm done to you or making up with the person who caused the harm. Forgiveness brings peace to your soul.

What are the effects of holding a grudge? They need to be looked at seriously because grudges have more impact on you than you think. If you're unforgiving, you might: bring anger and bitterness into every relationship and new experience, become so wrapped up in the wrong that you can't enjoy the present; right? become depressed or anxious; feel that your life lacks meaning or purpose; feel that you're at odds with your spiritual beliefs; lose valuable and enriching connectedness with others. There are serious consequences to not letting go and releasing these blockages.

How do you reach a state of forgiveness? Forgiveness is a commitment to a personalized process of change. To move from suffering to forgiveness, you might: recognize the value of forgiveness and how it can improve your life; identify what needs healing and who needs to be forgiven and for what; consider joining a support group or seeing a counselor; acknowledge your emotions about the harm done to you and how they affect your behavior and work to release them; choose to forgive the person who's offended you; move away from your role as victim and release the control and power the offending person and situation had in your life. As you let go of grudges, you'll no longer define your life by how you've been hurt. You might even find compassion and understandin .

"Holding onto anger is like drinking poison and expecting the other person to die"
Nelson Mandela

You can't be happy and sad at the same time. In order to move on, one has to let go of one of them and it may as well be the sad. You are the only one that even remotely cares about your past. Nobody cares about your past problems as much as you think. The only one who truly cares is you and you are torturing yourself by reliving it over and over again in your head day after day, week after week, month after month and year after year. It is only a story in your head now. The event is over and happened, you don't have a problem with the event anymore, you have a problem with yourself. **You can let it go and don't you know why.**

This is a critical point in your life becasue making the decision to rid yourself of your past will guide the rest of your life. It will be the best decision you ever make as you will be able to enjoy life all while extracting the torment and heartache that seems to never go away. You cannot protect yourself from your problems. Surrounding yourself in an environment that allows no one to touch the inner disturbance will only perpetuate and compound the problem. Your negative past or insecurities must be addressed and removed completely. We are all plagued with sensitivities about loneliness, rejection, our physical appearance, our mental aptitude- people swim in insecurities. We are walking around with a lot of fears that could explode at any given moment. If anyone brushes up against and ruffles these disturbances, you can become completely thrown off, causing you pain.

Let's say you are lonely so you now avoid going to places where couples tend to congregate. If you are afraid of rejection, you have to avoid getting too close to people. You have to adjust your life to make room for the inner disturbances to live on. This is the opposite of what must be done. You must remove these disturbances all together once and for all.

"Your restless soul is the culprit here, look inside yourself"

Let's say you are struggling with a drinking problem and don't want to drink anymore. This is a smart move but now you have to avoid anywhere that serves drinks or reminds you of drinking. You are making room for the inner disturbance to live on. Don't make room for it. Attack the insecurities head on and engage them. Look for situations where you can test your resolve and sharpen your skills. In this case, go to the bar and sit and listen to who you used to be. Listen to all the people at the bar who are all lubed up with alcohol, perhaps talking nonsense. Take a look at the old you and be ok with it. Look around while you are sipping on your green tea and realize the establishment has nothing to do with your drinking too much, your restless soul is the culprit here, look inside yourself.

Sit at the bar with a tall spine, shoulders back, chin up and a smile on your face telling yourself that you are in complete control of yourself, in control of how you behave and what goes into your mouth. Tell yourself you are in control of which thoughts you respond to, how you respond when you do decide to act. Tell yourself you are the one in control, not the location, not your friends, not your insecurities and certainly not the weakest part of your life, your past. "I am the steward of my life, I'm the boss here and I'll tell you when I drink and don't drink." Attacking the insecurities head on will serve to help you sharpen your skills and deepen your resolve towards the disturbance and its triggers. You must walk head-on into the disturbance with courage and fearlessness; it is the only way.

If you are telling yourself you are shy and lonely, go to a night club or bar and talk to people who are also there alone or even go out on a limb and talk with a group. Yeah, it will feel like having your molar teeth pulled out the first few outings. It will be bumpy in the beginning, a little rough in the middle but beautiful in the end. If you do this enough times, you will soon become good at small talk and then become comfortable speaking with people you have just met. This will lead you to getting to know people on the inside and the only way you can fall in love with someone is to know someone on the inside. Contextually, we are all the same; we all want the same things, and it is just the content that differs. Talk about the people you meet, ask them questions about themselves, you will be surprised how beautiful people are.

You will be amazed at how you can connect with anyone once you start to gather a few skills. Go to sporting events, go to church, sign up for painting class, go wherever people are and practice bringing your loneliness to its knees. Do this for a few months and I promise you, loneliness will slowly dissipate and eventually disappear. You will eventually start to wonder how in the world you could have spent all those years by yourself.

The Future

The other thing that smothers happiness is the mindless internal chatter about what we do not have and how are we going to get it. The uncertainty of the future and the perpetual thinking of how we are going to get to the future is a road block to happiness. Remember, the mind's job is to try to put the pieces of the puzzle together. Whatever you think, it must try to figure out how to get it. It has a constant desire to match what it wants with what it thinks; this can be a terrible burden on the mind.

People create unrealistic expectations that have almost no chance of being realized. You need to have the self-awareness to realize where you are and what you want. Realize that your mind is trying to bridge the gap between what you want and what you actually have. In most cases, this disconnect is so big that the mind has no idea how to bring these thoughts to fruition. If you want to go for a walk, the mind can very simply put this together, easy to figure out, "let's get off the couch and move our legs." The challenge is, the mind tells us that it needs things that are well beyond where you are right now in life. It is not that you can't have them it is just that the gap is too big right now and you have to start somewhere else. You want it all and you want it now. You are imposing too much upon yourself.

Most people have to take a step back at this point and realize who they are and where they are. Take stock in themselves, self-reflect and self-assess. You are placing unrealistic beliefs in place for yourself based on where you are today. Your mind is telling you that you want a supermodel girl/boyfriend, beautiful house, lake front recreational property, $100,000 car, private school for the kids, a nanny and a gardener, all while you're driving a $10,000 car and earning enough money to just get by. The mind has not the faintest clue on how to bridge this massive disconnect between your thoughts and reality. It doesn't know where to start and can begin to wrap in confusion.

"Happy people have modest and realistic levels of expectation and aspirations"

Overloading and burdening the mind with these types of disconnects will draw and suck up your natural energies and only serve to push you further away from happiness and contentment. Happy people have modest and realistic levels of expectation and aspirations. Happy people become happier when they toil away for years striving to accomplish a goal. Happy people accomplish one goal and move on to the next until they have stacked up years of little victories. Once you stack one modest aspirational win on top of another win for a couple of years, your life changes for the better. Always remember that happiness comes from the pursuit as well as the accomplishment.

Much of our time is thinking of the future. People spend too much time thinking about what they don't have and it draws the energy away from today and the moment. The moment we become content with what we have and who we are, the empty feeling of not knowing the future slowly goes away, keeping the goal of happiness closer. In order to get where you are going, you must be happy where you are. This is the great gift of gratitude. Once you become grateful for what you have, the portal to abundance opens wide and gives more of itself.

As we age, life and negative events can take their toll on us physically and emotionally. Divorce, business failure, death, betrayal, bankruptcy, addiction, the list goes on. Consider yourself lucky if you have only had one of these events happen in your life. These far from happy events take a toll on our spirit and weigh greatly on our minds. These negative events push us into the opposite direction of where we want to go which is towards happiness. Those of us who have been hit with these major events, some more than one at a time, can relate to this feeling of emptiness and loss. After people have been hurt enough times by life, spirits can weaken and attempts to grow can become futile. Here is the trick.

Regardless of how you were hurt or why your valley is so deep, you have to start digging your way out, you have to start your rise. **There are no options**. You must start somewhere. You must start where you are, with what you have and however you feel. Here is the time to tuck away the ego, roll up your sleeves and start grinding. One good day, 7 days in a row becomes a great week, put 4 of those weeks together and you have a super month. Twenty four months in a row creates powerful change in people. Think about it, two years and you can be a completely different person. Inspiring those around you, your children, family and friends. Living a life that is close to your dreams is only two years of hard work away minimum. I believe most people can acquire 75% of their desires in two years and most can accomplish their dreams in the fi e to ten year range. The biggest challenge with starting is that no one wants to be seen starting at the bottom. People believe that certain things are below them. They would rather continue to suffer than to get their hands dirty and make a plan and get after it. Keep in mind this one fact; a 10% percent change over time yields a 300% return. Don't be the type of person who prefers a known hell to and unknown heaven.

"After people have been hurt enough times by life, spirits can weaken and attempts to grow can become futile"

Assuming you are not a monk who needs nothing to be happy, happiness has a price tag and the price tag is working. It can be working to make money, working on yourself through reading and exercise, working on your plan, working on your legacy, your appearance, your character, your vocabulary, your community and the world at large. The price tag to happiness is working and sometimes you're starting at the bottom. A lot of the time there is no other way, and remember this: no one is keeping track, monitoring or caring in any way about whether you are succeeding, failing, winning, losing, or are even at bat. No one cares, zero people. So stop worrying about what other people are thinking because they aren't thinking about you, period. No one cares about how you feel or cares about your emotions so stop thinking that anyone does. Start attacking your insecurities and make a plan to get to the place you want to be.

Remember that happiness is all about having your thoughts, your words and your actions be the same. Don't let yourself down and happiness can be yours eternally. If you are having some trouble matching thoughts with appropriate actions, there are a couple of options. You can either impose more of your will into the world through direct action to get what you want or you can simply desire less. Whatever choice you make will immediately bring you closer to happiness.

Happiness is a skill, but it is a skill that has many components, and each of those components is a constructive way of being. Happy people are way ahead of others as science has proven over the last 20 years. A few of the advantages that happier people have are:

- Live longer on average, up to 10 years more.

- Make better and faster decisions.

- Have stronger immune systems and endure pain better.

- Are more satisfied with their jobs, are more productive, earn more, get rich more.

- Have less depression and suicide, greater self-control and coping skills.

- Are more successful

- Are more popular, more loved

- Have better relationships

- Have more friends, bigger social circle

- Have more pleasant and satisfying marriages

- Have better physical health

- Are mentally stronger, yet calmer

- Are kinder and help others more

- Are better and more regarded as leaders

"Bring happiness to every encounter in life, instead of expecting external events to create happiness"

You may have a long list of goals that you believe will provide you with contentment when they are achieved, yet if you examine your state of happiness in this moment, you will notice that the fulfillment of some previous ambitions didn't create an enduring sense of joy. Desires can produce anxiety, stress and competitiveness. It is important to acknowledge this. Bring happiness to every encounter in life, instead of expecting external events to create happiness. By staying true to yourself and in harmony with yourself, all the contentment you could ever dream of will begin to fl w into your life. The right people, the right opportunities, the necessary factors will come together. Stop pushing and pulling and feel grateful for what is.

It is often said that people spend the best years of their life trying to make money, sacrificing their health and their family only to spend the rest of their days paying that same money in an attempt to recover their lost health and their estranged family. If it is happiness you seek and aren't quite sure how to go about gathering it in, below are a few suggestions.

Exercise

Exercise has such a profound effect on our happiness and well-being that it is an effective strategy for overcoming depression. You don't have to be depressed to benefit from exercise though. Exercise can help you relax, increase your brain power, and improve your body image even if you don't lose any weight. Happiness is directly tied to exercise. As the brain releases proteins and endorphins, they make us feel happier.

Even if your actual appearance doesn't change, how you *feel* about your body does change.

Sleep More

You will have more positivity. We know that sleep helps our body recover from the day and repair itself and that it helps us focus and be more productive. It turns out sleep is also important for happiness. Sleep affects positivity, sleep deprivation hits the hippocampus harder than the amygdala. The result is that sleep-deprived people fail to recall pleasant memories yet recall gloomy memories just fin . Sleep also affects our sensitivity to negative emotions. Those who worked through the afternoon without taking a nap became more sensitive to negative emotions like fear and anger. Of course, how well and how long you sleep will probably affect how you feel when you wake up, which can make a difference to your whole day.

Spend More Time with Friends/Family

If you want more evidence that time with friends is beneficial for you, research proves it can make you happier right now. Social time is highly valuable when it comes to improving our happiness, even for introverts. We are happy when we have family, we are happy when we have friends and almost all the other things we think make us happy are actually just ways of getting more family and friends. The truth is we could increase our annual income by hundreds of thousands of dollars and still not be as happy as we would if we increased the strength of our social relationships. Money can't buy you happiness.

Get Outside More

Spending 20 minutes outside in good weather not only boosted positive mood, but broadened thinking and improved working memory. This is pretty good news for those of us who are worried about fitti g new habits into our already-busy schedules. Twenty minutes is a short enough time to spend outside that you could fit it into your commute or even your lunch break. Being outdoors, near the sea, on a warm, sunny weekend afternoon is the perfect spot for most. In fact, research study participants were found to be substantially happier outdoors in all natural environments than they were in urban environments.

Help Others

One of the most counterintuitive pieces of advice I found is, that to make yourself feel happier, you should help others. Helping someone else in anything brings immediate satisfaction. If you are feeling a little low go out and help someone. Shovel a driveway if it's snowing, volunteer at a food bank, help someone elderly cross the street; there are many opportunities to help people.

Practice Smiling

Smiling can make us feel better, but it's more effective when we back it up with positive thoughts. Of course it's important to practice "real smiles" where you use your eye sockets. We have all seen fake smiles that don't reach the person's eyes. Try it. Smile with just your mouth. Then smile naturally; your eyes narrow. There's a huge difference in a fake smile and a genuine smile. Smiling can improve our attention and help us perform better on cognitive tasks. Smiling makes us feel good which also increases our mental flexibility and our ability to think from our hearts. A smile is also a good way to reduce some of the pain we feel in troubling circumstances. Smiling is one way to reduce the distress caused by an upsetting situation. Even forcing a smile when we don't feel like it is enough to lift our mood slightly. It can be like push starting a car with a dead battery!

Meditate

"Research even shows that regular meditation can permanently rewire the brain to raise levels of happiness"

Rewire your brain for happiness. Meditation is often touted as an important habit for improving focus, clarity, and attention span, as well as helping to keep you calm. It turns out it's also useful for improving your happiness. Meditation literally clears your mind and calms you down, it's often been proven to be the single most effective way to live a happier life. Studies show that in the minutes right after meditating, we experience feelings of calm and contentment as well as heightened awareness and empathy. Research even shows that regular meditation can permanently rewire the brain to raise levels of happiness. The fact that we can actually alter our brain structure through mediation is most surprising to me and somewhat reassuring that however we feel and think today isn't necessarily permanent.

Move Closer to Work

Less commute equals being happier. Our commute to

work can have a surprisingly powerful impact on our happiness. The fact that we usually commute twice a day at least fi e days a week makes it unsurprising that the effect would build up over time and make us less and less happy. While many voluntary conditions don't affect our happiness in the long term because we acclimate to them, people never get accustomed to their daily slog to work because sometimes the traffic is awful and sometimes it's not. Living closer to work minimizes the negative stress that comes with commuting.

Practice Gratitude

This is a seemingly simple strategy but I've personally found it makes a huge difference to my outlook. There are lots of ways to practice gratitude, from keeping a journal of things you're grateful for to sharing good things that happen each day with a friend. In an experiment where participants took note of things they were grateful for each day, their moods were improved just from this simple practice.

Getting Older Will Actually Make You Happier

As we get older, particularly past middle age, we tend to naturally grow happier. The only way we can learn about life and the people in it is to be on the earth and live for a while. Time is guaranteed to throw us so many curveballs that we are certain to learn. With wisdom comes happiness. As we age, we tend not to place the same importance on things that we did with a less mature mind. Age changes our perceptions and attitudes, slowing down the mind, which brings with it peace.

TAKEAWAYS

- We must learn how to be happy and in a peaceful state of being. Happiness is not our natural state.

- Life will not always be the way you want it to be. That's okay.

- Colour and live outside the lines, it's ok to take risks; we must learn to jump.

- Circumstances are just that. Circumstances are not who you are. It is your perception of the circumstances that count.

- We create our own lows or valleys in life and they can be avoided.

- Once we are at peace and happy in our minds, the portal of the universe opens allowing in all of the things we desire. In this state, the universe will then listen to the nature of your song.

- We don't need to look anywhere else but inside. Happiness is not external and cannot be found from external sources.

- You must work at being happy. It takes effort, but the payoffs are substantial.

CHAPTER 3
RAISING HAPPY ADULTS

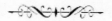

As children, we were steered and built by the direction of our parents, our school system, our teachers, friends and society at large. A child's life is like a piece of paper in which every person leaves a mark, which is why children need to be crafted from an early age, then let go.

Up to a certain point, children are completely creative and use their imagination to its fullest, that is, until we get to school. This is when we have to start thinking inside the systems and the teacher's boxes. Yes, we need to know math, science and a certain set of skills required to move forward in the world but our creativity is often thwarted inside the walls of classrooms. If you tell a child a few times, in a stern manner, not to do something, guess what? They will stop doing it that way. Their brain will then continue to reason in this way for all sorts of things that are life. This channels or funnels them into the mindset that there is something that is right and something wrong. Instead we need to simply let the children fig re out "their" way.

Why? Because we are told, "grow up", "that is silly", "don't do it that way", "be quiet", "who do you think you are", "don't color outside the lines" and all that stuff. When you are a kid in school and you become restless and want to move around or speak your mind, you're told to "settle down" or "you can't do it that way" or "don't disrupt the class". Who says we can't do it that way? Our teachers, families and our friends. All the most important and influential people that surround us daily and shape who we become. We really shouldn't be hearing these messages as formative children whose minds are like sponges. I'm not saying let the kids run roughshod and yes of course, if little Johnny is in danger, he needs to be told not to do it that way, but short of that let's let our children figure it out on their own without influenc . Guide them in the right directions but don't micro manage them. Experience can be the best teacher.

The message we should be teaching our children is do whatever and whichever way you want and you will eventually figure out what works. You see, once you make all the necessary mistakes, you will know what not to do the next time. This attitude also leads to tremendous creativity. Creativity that is free fl wing and designed form the moment of inception. It is not blocked or altered by anyone.

"Once you make all the necessary mistakes, you will know what not to do the next time"

As we age, we become totally disoriented in our own environment. We can become like a mixed bag of contrasting perceptions and beliefs about the world. This comes from the all of the people who have influenecd you as you were raised. Let me tell you that some of these beliefs, opinions and perception are wrong and in a lot of cases, misguided. These formative perceptions of life can become engrained in us and not evolve as needed while we age. Be careful when listening to Uncle Johnny or Aunt Sally because if you were able to look into their lives they haven't figu ed it out either. It can be a case of the blind leading the blind.

Even though we have been given the mental faculties to create our own environment, we don't. We are no longer like the chipmunk that within days of birth, is scrambling around with agility and confidenc . We are no longer the giraffes loping around the field days after birth. We can become confused and weak within, creating an outside world that is fearful and cautious. Where we should be striding like a lion, we scamper like sheep.

First, we are taught as children to takes risks, fall down and don't worry because this is how you learn to walk and live. Then once we get to a certain age, we are taught and told that, "that will take forever to complete", "that's too risky", "I would be careful with that one", "no one in our family has done that so you should try something else that is easier" and "color inside the lines, you don't want to be messy". "Look how Jane did it, she colored inside the lines, and you should be more like Jane".

I don't know why but a shift starts to take place that takes us away from the "risk taking" mentality to the "be safe and don't get hurt" mentality. This is the first step that begins to discombobulate us as to how great we can be. **This is the first stage to stunted growth.** Parents, teachers, friends and society: do children a favour, watch over them with your love but don't interfere with their growth and happiness in life. Do not micromanage them through the perceptions you learned from your parents. Try another way, let them develop their own perceptions and belief systems. Guide them from long term and permanent damage, but do not be afraid to let them fail.

Did you know the school curriculum in Finland revolves around the children having little to no homework and only are taught how to enjoy themselves and play around for most of the day in order to develop happiness? In Finland, the main goal for the children is to make sure they are enjoying themselves. The teachers will follow the children around all day and continuously ask them if they are enjoying themselves and playing as much as they can. They want these children to use their imaginations as much as possible and not shut down the creative minds that are so brilliant and yet underused. Did you know that this school system has the highest marks of all schools and these children go on to be the most satisfied adults where they are the happiest and fulfilled? Did you know that **Finland is always at the top of the charts for the best places to live in the world?**

The transformation of the Finns' education system began some 40 years ago as the key propellant of the country's economic recovery plan. Educators had little idea it was so successful until 2000, when the first results from the Program for International Student Assessment (PISA), a standardized test given to 15-year-olds in more than 40 global venues, revealed Finnish youth to be the best young readers in the world. Three years later, they led in math. By 2006, Finland was first out of 57 countries (and a few cities) in science. "I'm still surprised," said Arjariita Heikkinen, principal of a Helsinki comprehensive school. "I didn't realize we were *that* good."

There are no mandated standardized tests in Finland, apart from one exam at the end of students' senior year in high school. There are no rankings, no comparisons or competition between students, schools or regions. Finland's schools are publicly funded. The people in the government agencies running them, from national officials to local authorities, are educators, not business people, military leaders or career politicians. Every school has the same national goals and draws from the same pool of university-trained educators.

The result is that a Finnish child has a good shot at getting the same quality education no matter if he or she lives in a rural village or a university town. Ninety-three percent of Finns graduate from academic or vocational high schools, 17.5 percentage points higher than the United States, and 66 percent go on to higher education, the highest rate in the European Union. Yet Finland spends about 30 percent less per student than the United States.

"We have no hurry, children learn better when they are ready. Why stress them out?"

Teachers in Finland spend fewer hours at school each day and spend less time in classrooms than American teachers. Teachers use the extra time to build curriculums and assess their students. Children spend far more time playing outside, even in the depths of winter. Homework is minimal. Compulsory schooling does not begin until age 7. "We have no hurry," said Heikkinen "Children learn better when they are ready. Why stress them out?" Does this sound familiar North American parents? We want to jam little Johnny into hockey at 4 years old and have him training 4-5 days a week by 8 years old, because he will be the next professional hockey player. Let's put Cindy in dance, piano, pre-kindergarten education and we should have her singing as well by the time she is 7.

It's almost unheard of for a child to show up hungry or homeless in Finland. The state provides three years of maternity leave and subsidized day-care to parents, and preschool for all 5-year-olds, where the emphasis is on play and socializing. In addition, the state subsidizes parents, paying them around 150 euros per month for every child until he or she turns 17.

Ninety-seven percent of 6-year-olds attend public preschool, where children begin some academics. Schools provide food, medical care, counseling and taxi service if needed. Student health care is free.

We are taught in our school system to be conforming and to be prepared for a certain employment once complete. We are taught that once we have this employment we shall be happy and satisfied. It should be the other way around. We should be taught to be happy and satisfied and creative and then we shall find the passion that will eventually lead to the employment that makes us the money that we need to live in this world. This is what makes happy people. People who are making money doing the things they love to do. Unhappy people are people who are doing things they don't like and making small amounts of money.

At school, we should be taught to figure it out on our own. This is the foundation of the Finnish school curriculum. Find out what it is like to climb a tree, find out what it feels like to fall off the monkey bars, see what it is like to be silent for a period of time. Let them figure out how to find the best way for them. This seems counterintuitive but in the long run, this develops creativity, common sense and strong reasoning abilities. The problem is that in the short term the kids are seen as trouble a nuisances or disruptive. Mom and Dad have things to do, they are busy, perhaps already frustrated and in their own heads with all of their problems. Do you think they have the time, the patience or the understanding to sit back and listen to little Johnny work through all of his challenges? No chance. Instead Johnny is told to tow the line, sit down, be quiet and relax. This happens from the minute a child wakes up and goes to school to the time he goes to bed, all day, every day, always being told what to do.

Let the children play with no boundaries or preconceived ideas of what play is. Let them create on the fl , let them make the mistakes necessary to fi ure it out on their own. It prepares the kids for real life in different ways than our schools do. We as adults have to re-learn a lot of things and most of us aren't capable or simply don't want to spend the time relearning how to have peace of mind, joy and happiness, or we are unable to re-learn such concepts.

We need to teach our children how to be peaceful, happy and creative as the foundation to their being and their future. This is because their future selves will be the most productive and creative once they are peaceful, happy and internally fulfilled. I'm not saying to cradle the children and enable poor habits, but rather give them a longer leash. Don't be so quick to force your beliefs and opinions on them. Don't be so quick to jump into every situation and have to fix it or cater it to your likings.

"What happens is when children don't understand peace of mind, joy and happiness they become adults who don't understand peace of mind, joy and happiness"

Today's curriculum here in North America needs to be changed to ensure that children are given the best chance to succeed in the modern world. I don't see anyone switching to the Finnish Curriculum anytime soon but here are my suggestions on the changes required to build children who will turn into strong confident and enlightened adult .

Children must be taught the following:

The inner workings and motives of all people. This will

help them understand that we are all the same, giving them insight into better communication skills. When we realize that the other person is exactly as we are and wants the same things, it is much easier to communicate.

Teach children the power of thought habits and daily habits. Make sure children understand the law of manifestation: what you think is what resonates in you and is what you act on and eventually become.

Don't allow them to be consumed and suffocated by their thoughts. Help them to understand that they are the soul or the subconscious behind their thoughts. This is what happens to children when they don't know why they are thinking the way they are. After a while they can begin to think there is something wrong with them.

They must be taught the true nature of sex and its power to be used as a life strengthening tool. Not just you put this in there and a baby comes out. Sex is like food and water to humans. Let's make sure kids understand why they are thinking the way they are. They can become confused very easily.

Help children understand achievement and how people achieve greatness. This includes mindset, soul set, thought habits, daily habits, passion and patience over many years.

Show children the path that all of the greats in history have taken. They need to learn on a level they can relate to. Teach them about their parents and how they achieved. Teach them about current people who have achieved and leave the 300 year old explorers out of the content.

Tell them the massive importance love has in their lives. Teach them that they are love. Just like sex, love is a huge emotion that can be like a time bomb if not understood. They need to know all about love.

They need to understand that power and strength is in

compassion, kindness, love and a quiet mind; not in loud, aggressive, mean or dominating behaviour.

Children need to be taught how to eat properly and the impact food has on their bodies. They need to be shown that proper eating will lead to power, strength and confidenc .

It is very important that children are taught to slow down their minds. **They need quiet time.** 10-15 minutes a day with eyes closed and quiet. Being a child can be very confusing. If they are not taught that they are the stewards of their minds, it will perpetuate mindless thinking which manifests into its physical counterpart of mindless behaviour.

Teach children about budgeting and investment. Teach them about the banks and the purpose of financial institutions. Make sure they know about compound interest and what market investing looks like.

It is critical that children aren't absorbed into the constant negativity that surrounds them. They need to be taught how to combat this and stay happy. Remember, if a mind isn't corralled and harnessed, it becomes a wild mind, one that reacts to every thought. Dangerous and not in a good way.

Help them bridge the gap between what they hear from all sources around them and what is actually the truth of life. Children do not what is the truth is in many circumstances. They can very easily be lead astray by wrong information. The television, their friends, their teachers and their largest infl - ences can and do give them wrong and misguided information. This is why you need to explain the difference, otherwise it can become their reality.

Children need to learn that life isn't about gathering material items and looking a certain way to the world; it isn't about the fast car, the big house and the bling. Teach them the reverse; happiness, health and well-being will bring them all the material riches they could ever want.

Teach them how to colour outside the lines. Let them know that this is where their best self-resides.

Teach them how to recognize practical ideas and thoughts. Children have a mind just like adults; it is operating 24 hours a day. They need to be able to sift through the 60,000 thoughts they have in a day and hand pick the ones that give them inspiration that will eventually lead to whatever they demand of life.

Without knowing about success and failure, being a kid can be a long haul. Teach them that failure is expected and required and that if they aren't failing, then they aren't trying hard enough.

Don't let kids coast, they need physical activity and need to understand the value of working hard and diligently.

Teach children how massively important relationships are in our overall health, happiness and well-being. Teach them how to behave in relationships by showing them relationship skills. Children are slowly moving away from personal physical relationships and into the online world. This will have huge consequences based on what we know about the importance of close personal relationships and conflict management skills.

Let them understand that life is the great teacher through experience and that textbooks and schools are not the true teachers; it is life's experiences that are the biggest teachers.

Show them how to be accountable and to accept the facts of life the way they are. Accountability is king and is true strength. Teach them to not look for excuses, but accountability.

Children need to be true to themselves. Teach them that their job is to be the best version of themselves and no one else.

Teach them not to have loose opinions, to have opinions based on fact or close to it.

They need to know that acting on thought without proper

consideration can become a problem. In today's world, everyone wants it now. Children need to understand the dangers in this. Teach them long-term thinking.

The need to be taught that discipline equals freedom. If they are disciplined in life they will experience freedom in all facets of life. Discipline over time yields the results we desire.

We can do whatever it is we want, we just need to have the proper mindset and a game plan that is followed by perseverance and discipline. If we give the children the proper education, defined as the process of receiving or giving systematic instruction, especially at a school or University, I think we shall be pleasantly surprised. We owe them the minimization of disturbances.

So here we've got human beings, with marvelous minds, and they are struggling, thinking they are stuck with the conditions or circumstances by which they are surrounded. I'd like to do it but I can't because.... Whatever follows "because" is the circumstance they become subservient to the circumstance. The circumstance becomes their version of defeat and they do what their perception and circumstances dictate. They don't even try to come up with a better way.

Here is the point, when you go on to do something you have never done, where there are going to be all kinds of crazy things going on inside of you, there is going to be that little voice that says "Who do you think you are? You can't do that. You couldn't possibly write that book or whatever it is you are thinking of doing". This will turn into a battle and, more often than not, that little voice wins the conversation. **We create fear where there is none**. We fabricate difficulty for the sole purpose of misdirecting ourselves away from what we know we should be doing. The little voice says "what if I don't succeed," "what will people think if I fail," "I don't have the skills to do this." The excuses start pouring in and, in short order, you don't even start.

"The hardest part is the start." - *Don Shula, Hall of Fame NFL Coach*

The little voice goes on to justify the lack of action by telling itself that it probably wouldn't have worked anyway or it wasn't the best idea, all in the face of your gut and heart telling you that you would love to do it and what a joy it would be. The little voice will tell you that it will be too much work, too costly, take up too much time, too difficult. It will tell you whatever it needs to, in order for you not to act on your wants and desires. It will lie to you to think it is keeping you secure. Do yourself a favour and don't miss out on your passion in life because of a little voice that tells you that you can't do it. It can be done and all you need is the will, a plan, discipline and time.

Not starting something you are passionate about provides a negative momentum and gives you an escape for this endeavour and those to follow. I am telling you, no matter how big or small, the next time you think about doing something you want to do, simply go do it. Make a plan, gather the resources you need, develop a timeline and then do it. There will never be a good time and there will always be a boatload of excuses in your head you must overcome. The universal law of "success breeds success" can fl w freely in your life. It doesn't matter how big or small, just go do it.

In order to figure out how to change my life, I didn't have to study anyone else's life; all I did was study me. I don't have to study you, I just had to study me. We are all the same. Some are males, some are females but outside the reproductive system we are all the same. The only difference is appearance and the truth is rarely in the appearance of things. Use your higher faculties and look within.

We were taught that we needed to change things on the

outside. We seem to feel that the grass is greener somewhere else. Work on your inside faculties and your life will reach levels you couldn't have imagined. We are conditioned to live through our senses. We see, hear, smell, taste and touch. We let the outside world control our minds. We react to what people say and how people respond. We have all been blessed with higher mental faculties of intuition, perception, will, memory, reason, emotions and imagination. When we begin to develop these faculties, we can control our outside world and stop letting it control us.

Einstein was right when he said, "the intuitive mind is a sacred gift and the rational mind is a faithful servant. We have created a society that honours the servant and has forgotten the gift". What we need to do first is gain a realization that we were programmed from childhood, by our teachers, families, social media, and the media at large; then learn how we can change it so that it stops controlling us and we start controlling ourselves. That's when the fun starts and you become your own master. You cannot master anyone until you master yourself.

I am not a psychologist but I know that for some reason the path of least resistance and the easy way are the paths most taken. We all want the most for the least effort. Call it what it is. This just isn't possible for anyone. The laws of the universe simply don't permit it. The laws of the universe are the same for all of us. What we put in is what we get out. If we want love, we must love. Love doesn't come to people who are haters. If we want to be healthy and fit, we must exercise regularly. If we want a decent amount of money, we must work for it. The bible says, "you get what you give", and this is absolute truth. Don't question this for a second as it is one of the universal laws.

It is all inside of you already. You don't need to look anywhere else. We are all the same and you have inside of you what is required to get what you need out of this life and reach your destiny of fulfillment. We have been taught to think that the answers and our best life is somewhere else, somewhere outside of us. This is wrong, our best lives reside within us, deep within our minds. We simply need to take the time with ourselves to understand ourselves and unleash the beauty and power that lies within. Do not participate in the struggle, realize that the events that happen in the moment belong to the moment. They don't belong to you. Do not define yourself in relation to them, just let them come and go.

Once we become satisfied peaceful and content in our minds, we immediately begin to enjoy our best lives. Our best life is not around the corner, not impossible and certainly achievable. It will take some work, some perseverance and discipline. In order to understand yourself, you will have to learn about your mind and how it works so that you can get in touch with your inner power and strength.

How long have you been struggling to keep it all together? Anytime something happens that goes against the protective mental model you have built for and about yourself, you have to defend and rationalize to get it all back together. Your mind won't stop until you have found a way to justify and make it ok. People feel their very existence is at stake and will figh tooth and nail and argue until they get control back. The only reason for this is because we tried to build solidarity where there is none. Now we are always fighting to keep an imagined belief of ourselves together. The problem here is that there is no way out; this mentality will keep you perpetually trapped inside yourself. You must let go of fractured beliefs or you will always be defending yourself. This is a dangerous game that only leaves you having to keep everything and everybody straight in order to balance your conceptual model with reality.

My suggestion for elevating your life beyond reading this book, is to read books, listen to audio tapes and learn from our forefathers and mothers. **This is a lot easier than we think.** Millions of people have passed before with great success and it is incumbent upon us to learn from these people. The mind is a very powerful organ that controls our destiny so let's massage it with the most love we can.

TAKEAWAYS

- Our North American school curriculum has to be upgraded bringing it in line with what we know already is best for them.

- Happy children become happy adults. Let's build some happy children, everybody wins.

- Don't stymie children with negative thoughts, actions and words. Happy children can be shaped at an early age quite easily with the key being consistency.

- The happier you are the better is the quality of your life.

- Don't be in such a hurry; children learn best when they are ready, why stress them out?

- We have to start teaching our children differently immediately. We have evolved over the last 100 years and now know better than we did before. Let's upgrade the parenting and school curriculum to be current with our times.

- Don't be tricked by your conniving mind. When moments of inspiration arise, jump on them and act with vigor. Don't give your mind enough time to talk you out of doing it. Be ALL IN!!!!!!

CHAPTER 4

ALWAYS OPPOSITES- CAUSE AND EFFECT

There is always an effect to an action or lack of action. There is always a result to forward motion or backward motion or no motion at all. There are consequences to actions or lack thereof. People do all sorts of things in life: build businesses, meditate, make music, invest in themselves, read, journal, exercise, make movies, travel, ride horses, work. People are always doing stuff; it's what we do. We are all doing something all of the time during our waking hours. We really have no option because we can only sleep for so long until the brain wakes up and won't allow further sleep.

While awake, we roam the earth deciding how to fill up our time. These decisions day after day, week after week, year after year create who we are, determines our existence and our future. Daily decisions compound over time, much like money compounds with interest over time. Each one of the hundreds of decisions made daily have an effect on the quality of your life. It is the same for everyone; it is our fate. Our daily decisions and habits create who we are.

On the contrary, people also choose not to do very much at all with themselves, surf the couch, watch lots of TV, eat unhealthily, lack passion, avoid exercise, speak negatively and not work on themselves. There is nothing wrong with this. How we choose to live our lives is entirely up to us. There is no right way of living and no wrong way, it's just life. What we need to be aware of though is energy must go somewhere whether as action or not. This energy is who you are and what makes your life. Energy is the source foundation of all life whether it is being used or not being used. Whether it is good, bad indifferent, lazy, active, sleepy, energetic, negative, optimistic, happy or sad, whatever and however you choose to live doesn't make a difference to the universe but it should make a difference to you.

What you choose to do, what you choose to eat, what you choose to say and how you choose to spend each day is who you are. You and the universe will only act by the way of natural laws. If you are filled with anxiety and anger that is what you will get back. If you roam the earth with joy and contentment, you will receive back joy and contentment. You can't possibly expect to walk around complaining being angry and bitter and have Prince Charming come sweep you off your feet. If you want to find a special person, get a great job or simply lift your internal status be sure you are doing the work inside, becoming special. The more you invest in self-mastery the more valuable of a person you become and as a result, the more you have to offer the world.

We have looked at how easy it is to design yourself with no opposition from anyone or anything; it's just a choice like any other. If you haven't already, make sure you know exactly who you want to be as of today and intimately know the characteristics that make up that person. It is imperative to know your character because it will be tested over and over with life and the people in it.

"The more you invest in self-mastery the more valuable of a person you become and as a result, the more you have to offer the world"

From the minute your eyes open in the morning you are faced with decision after decision. What do I wear? What do I eat? Which way should I drive to work? Should I go to the gym? Should I call Gail? Should I get coffee or tea? Do I cut the grass? Should I watch a movie? And on and on for 100 years if you're lucky enough to live that long. The decisions you make every day become your life, it is that simple. Humans make 35,000 decisions a day. If you live to a solid age of 80, that equals over a billion decisions you will make in your life-time. Each decision has a compound effect on your life, on who you are and what your future is.

Take these daily decisions very seriously. Some of these decisions will result in things you want and conversely some will result in undesirable outcomes; that's life for all of us. Imagine what can be done if you start to make different decisions each day, each morning each night. If you change a few little things in your daily decision making, it can have tremendous impact on your life in the short and long term. Did you know that if you added an extra 3 hours a day for yourself, let's say you get up at 5 am instead of 8 am, 5 days a week (not weekends) and did that for 40 years, you would have added 3.28 years of 24 hours per day to work on yourself? You would have added 28,800 hours to your life to do whatever you want. All for the simple sacrifice of going to bed a little earlier and rising a little earlier. Imagine all of the tasks or projects or dreams you could accomplish with 24 hours a day for 3.28 years.

Let's look at what everyone wants in some form or another. We all, more or less, want the same stuff on Earth: health, energy, love, peace of mind, material items, family, purpose, spirituality and happiness. There might be a few derivatives of these but, essentially, that is what we all can access and obtain with our worldly endeavours and efforts. In other words, everybody wants these things, including you. We all make the most of our decisions with one of these favourable outcomes in mind. We believe that, if we can have all of this stuff in abundance, we shall be fulfilled and content. Well you're right, this is exactly how you will feel when you have all of these things in abundance. How could you not feel great with an abundance of love, happiness, material items, passion, health, spirituality, family and great energy? You will be over the moon happy should you have an abundance of all of these things. Here-in lies the main issue with most people. We want all of these things but some of us aren't doing what is necessary to get them.

"The number one factor that separates high achievers vs. low or average achievers is consistency"

People's daily habits don't match their desires and they become frustrated and anxious when they don't get the abundance. It is almost like they expect to have it all for as little effort as possible. There are no free passes here. If you want the abundance, there is a price tag and it comes in the form of daily habits, patience and self-discipline executed with consistency over years.

You would be surprised to know that the number one factor that separates high achievers vs. low or average achievers is consistency. That's it, mystery solved. Don't quit when it gets hard, don't quit when it doesn't go your way, don't quit when you don't see the results quite yet, don't quit when it gets dark or cold, don't quit when you tired and aren't seeing the love, the money, the success. It`s over when you win and not until then!

While work is required, it is much easier than it seems to gather up the abundance. The first step is complete, you have made it this far. As you continue to read, the path will soon reveal the light. Right about the time when you reach enlightenment is about when all of the God-given abundance begins to show up in your life. Keep an eye open for these moments. When they happen, realize exactly why. It`s because your heart and soul have no weight, both are unblocked and now a true portal for fl w and opportunity. It is because your mind has settled down and quieted and isn't in control anymore. You have taken a seat in your soul. **You've gotten out of your own way.** You have been able to see events in life occur in front of you giving them no energy or resistance. Everything comes by pure design now, nothing comes without deep consideration. Enlightenment is reserved only for those who expect it, receive it, respect it, treasure it and pay it forward.

On the other side of cause and effect is the effect that occurs from poor decision-making. Eating the wrong foods, speaking poorly, complaining, being negative and engaging in negativity, not working hard, being lazy, lacking purpose, not testing or investing in yourself, being anti-social and thinking poorly.

These decisions over time create a person most people wouldn't be proud of. We all know these people, they are everywhere. Don't mistake my intentions, if you are lazy, unengaged, complaining, void of energy and are happy, then don't change a thing, happiness and fulfillment is the end game. If these qualities make you happy, then all is good. For those who aren't happy being where they are and realizing there is better, the path is ready for your entry. Once you are on the path, much force will be required to pull you off.

In a lot of cases people are forced to change because their current daily choices have interfered with their body temple and broken the body or mind. We see this with heart disease, high cholesterol, poor sleep, obesity, fatigue and energy levels, anxiety, restlessness, depression and disease. Make the right decisions now before it is too late and they are made for you. No one starts out to be this way; it takes years and years of the same daily decisions, then one day we look in the mirror and Bam!, there we are, not really what we had in mind. This is the culmination of years and years of poor decisions. Thought habits are forces that hold the destinies of men and women.

It is clear without question that the difficulty in which people find themselves are of their own making. More than that, their difficulties are seldom the outgrowth of immediate circumstances. They are generally a culmination of series of circumstances which have been consolidated through untrained habits and thoughts. The good news is that it can be undone.

"Thought habits are forces that hold the destinies of men and women"

Becoming overweight takes years of effort, damaging your lungs with smoke takes years of smoking, developing a bad attitude takes years of seeing negative people, cirrhosis of the liver requires years of abuse, decaying teeth the same.

Bodies and minds take years to break down and in most cases the good news is they can be fi ed. These decaying scenarios are the result of the many decisions that were made.

Take the time and really examine your daily decision-making. Your daily habits and decisions become who you are. Nothing will change day to day but when you look back over a year or two, everything changes. Make sure you make consistent pushes forward at any cost, keep getting small daily victories because they stack up and one day appear as a major victory. The importance of solid daily habits cannot be underestimated. At an absolute minimum, good daily habits will keep you healthy and happy. At a maximum, they will give you everything you desire and have dreamed of. Have a look inside and let the answers to the questions below join into your soul set.

Am I friendly? Do I smile and how often? Do I eat well consistently? Am I peaceful? What time do I go to bed? Who are my close friends? Do I spend time in nature? How much fun do I have? What's my weight? Do people like me? Do strangers approach me often or ever? Do I laugh often? Could I be more fun? Do I invest in myself on any level? Do I take time for me first? Am I happy? Do I deserve to be happy? Could I make more money? Am I passionate about life? Would I like to change or tweak a few things about me?

Where you are today is a direct result of all the millions of decisions that you have made up to this point. Here is the best part. If you are unsatisfied, take a look inside, take a look at your daily habits. This is where the answer lies. If you want to improve yourself, you can, and it won't be as hard as you think. Design your daily habits around the person that you believe you are and where you want to be. Remember that "new you" you created in the last chapter? It's time to put that person to the test through the paces of disciplined daily habits.

This is the only way to change or design you, this is the only way out. Don't think this is different for anyone else on planet Earth. Nobody is magically healthy, vibrant and strong. People make themselves; they create who they are. Conversely no one is magically 50 lbs. overweight, bitter and lonely. These scenarios take years to come to fruition. As long as it took for the person to be healthy and strong, it took the same amount of time to get 50 lbs. overweight. I refer to this as **doubling your workload.**

"Nothing will change day to day but when you look back over a year or two, everything changes"

Let's look at the person 50 lbs. overweight. They have to do double the work to reach the person who is fit and healthy. They must first lose the 50lbs and then work the identical amount if not more to get the nice body and strength they wish to have. Had they just kept all the unnecessary foods out of their mouths they wouldn't have to lose the 50 lbs. and they could start at ground zero. If that person didn't spend so much time around negative people and become negative themselves, they could start to be happy immediately instead of having to rid their lives of the blockages and negativity first. If we don't start the bad habits in the first place, we can start at ground zero which is the best place to start. You can look at it exactly like taking on too much financial debt. The minute you get money, you have to pay everyone first before you can pay yourself, instead of making the money and investing it where it can make you more money.

After working with so many people and personally living the highs and lows of life, being in the peaks and the valleys, having achievement and feeling disappointment, enjoying the wins and losses and being weak at the extremes, I wondered if it would be easier to exist in a middle ground where things are a bit more even keeled. Maybe a place that didn't make me feel like I was in a washer and dryer all the time being tumbled around. I began to wonder if there was a place without all the highs and lows. As I wrote this book, I kept hearing about the special place called the "middle ground", a place of reprieve, a place where we can rest, a place that isn't too high and isn't too low with limited up and downs. It became my understanding that there is a place where there are no extremes.

This intrigued me greatly as it was exactly what I had been looking for and writing about for the past year and half. As I began to learn more, this middle ground began to give rise within me, it became very clear that there was a sanctuary of reprieve. A place where the mind could slow down and take a well-deserved breather. It turns out this is a well walked path, not only by me but by millions before me. I started to wonder why, at some point along the way, in school, or at home or with friends, was I not taught about the middle ground? How could these hallowed grounds be hidden from me the whole time? It was never shown to me, brought to my attention nor had I ever heard anyone speak of it. Perhaps I wasn't ready or I wasn't looking hard enough but whatever the case, I knew I was on to something much bigger than me. So I pushed forward with faith, knowing the path was the right one.

People have been speaking and writing of the middle ground for thousands of years. It is the foundation of the enlightened. This finding was the validation I needed to keep writing and understanding how powerful the mind is and how much of a true joy this life can be. This sacred place of calmness, peace, joy and enlightenment has been a mystical place until now. It has always seemed that enlightenment was reserved only for other wiser people. Entry into enlightenment is for any human being to use to their advantage, anyone can get in. The term enlightenment almost seems unattainable and reserved only for those who sit on mountain tops in robes for years on end.

"Being a human being permits you entry to this higher state"

You don't need to change your clothes or sit in the lotus position for days to reach enlightenment. Being a human being permits you entry to this higher state. In getting there you will need to understand about the ego. The ego is a big deal. The ego is made up of six parts that account for how we experience ourselves disconnected from our core authenticity. If you allow the ego to determine your life's path you deactivate your authentic self. If you allow your ego to run your life you move further and further away from the centre.

Here are the six ego beliefs that you need to remove from your psyche:

1. I am what I have. My material items define m .

2. I am what other people think of me. My reputation defines m .

3. I am what I do. The things I have achieved along the way define m .

4. I am separate from everyone. My body defines me as alone

5. I am separate from all that is missing in my life. My life space is disconnected from my desires.

6. I am separate from God. My existence depends on assessment or judgement from God

You will feel the pulls of the ego and will recognize them immediately because you will hear your voice thinking on one of the above. Don't pay too much attention to the ego, it is very powerful but you can handle it. We have been gifted with the ability of self-control.

As I kept reading into the depths of what the middle ground is, it turns out that there are many philosophies surrounding the middle ground. We shall have a look at two of the bigger ones here.

Tao Teachings

These teachings are revered by many and only used by some. Summing up the Taoist philosophy on the middle ground is difficult but I think you will understand the core concept through this passage.

"Under heaven all can see beauty as beauty, only because there is ugliness. All can know good as good only because there is evil. Being and not being produce each other. The difficult is born in the easy. Long is defined by short, the high by the low. Before and after go along together. So the saje lives open with duality and paradoxical unity. The saje can work without effort and teach without words. Nurturing things without possessing them. He works not for rewards, he competes not for results, when the work is done it is forgotten. That is why it lasts forever."

The Tao is the middle ground that is in between the opposites or extremes, where nothing is pushing or pulling. It is a realization that there always are opposites of everything and the middle is where the Tao lives. The Tao tells us to stay away from the extremes because the extremes take up way too much of our time and energy. People waste too much time at the extremes. There are lots of examples of extreme but the underlying premise is stay away from the extremes because they become full time projects that will consume a good portion of your life. The more extreme it is, the more time you spend on it.

> *"The Tao is the middle ground that is in between the opposites or extremes, where nothing is pushing or pulling"*

Let's use the food example because it is relatable to all of us. Let's say you should only eat a certain amount of food in order to stay healthy and you choose to eat way too much food for way too long and now you are overweight or even obese. If you choose to stay this way, you have to spend a disproportional amount of energy and time keeping your "weight" alive by feeding it. You have to go to the store more often, spend more money, think about it more, cook more, digest longer and sleep more. It's a lot of stuff and takes up a lot of time. This is living in the extreme. Same goes for someone who is drinking too much at the extreme. The amount of effort it takes to be an alcoholic is nothing short of spectacular. Alcoholics spend a lot of time dealing with this extreme. Buying it, drinking it, thinking about it, lying about it, feeling awful, sleeping, headaches, lethargy, loneliness, highs and lows that are on the extreme. It is truly amazing some of the stuff we voluntarily put ourselves through.

Living at the extremes depletes the only energy source you have; it robs you of your natural vitality. Living in the extremes causes people to surrender the sovereignty of their lives. The extremes apply to spouses yelling at each other or being in a terrible relationship. Also true for drugs, sex, sleep, loneliness, gossiping etc. Do not spend any more time in the extremes; it takes up all of your energy, time and effort and in the end, we get nothing of great return. The return on investment (ROI) is always negative when in the extremes. Extremes cause an imbalance. Stay away from unbalanced ground and enjoy the comforts and relaxation of the middle ground.

The inefficiency of your actions and life is directly related to how many degrees off centre you are. You will notice when you are drawn off center that you will feel gentle pulls inside of yourself. It will start with your thoughts going off centre followed by a little tug inside with a possible shot of adrenaline. This is when the process of moving off centre begins. Just like grabbing onto great ideas and running with them, you can grab onto bad ideas and run with them. Bad ideas or thoughts can very quickly take you off course. This is your moment to right the ship, bail out any water you have taken on. The moment your thoughts start to go off centre will be very evident to you. You will know because they are your thoughts. If they keep arriving in your mind pay special attention and make sure you steer ALL energy away from them. Surf the bad ideas briefly and let them crash to shore, gone forever. Let the thoughts move through you and not get stuck in your psyche to the point where they cause you to act. If you are not able to stop the process in its tracks, you will begin to attach emotion to the event. Once this occurs you will give thought to it more and more; you will begin to give it life.

"The return on investment (ROI) is always negative when in the extremes"

Should you continue to allow the disturbance to move deeper inside of you, it will seep into your heart and then directly into your soul. Once there, it will have consumed you; it is even further downhill from here. It can cling and be stuck in you for days, months and even years controlling your every move. Stop it in its tracks; do not allow it to change the course of your life for the worse. Be vigilant and guard the gates of your mind with all the willpower you can muster up. You are the first and only line of defence so strap on the helmet and get ready for some knocks. Always remember, the predominating thought that has emotion attached to it is the one acted upon first. Stop the thought nonsense the moment it comes in.

If you don't stop giving life to the unwanted thoughts in the first ten or so seconds, you run the risk of further danger. **These first ten seconds are critical.** If you can't shut the perception and emotion attached to this event down in short order it will steal your time and energy, slowly consuming you. The problem here is you won't be able to use your energy for proper living. This is because your thoughts, your energy and your time will be deployed to attend to the emotional event you've chosen to cling to.

Deploying all of your energy into the event at the extreme only serves to rob you of that same energy that you could be using to design your great life. What you choose to give your energy towards is the most important of all choices you are required to make. You can't allow the "thought of the day" to interfere with your purpose, direction and plan.

Should you choose the middle ground, you will tap into a well of energy that you didn't know was available. You will have rid yourself of all of the mental nonsense that you deal with on a regular basis and now have all this free time to do so many other things, like design your magical life. This is the reward of the middle ground. People who walk the middle ground are rewarded with peace, stillness, less stress, more free time, bigger smiles, more money, more happiness and better overall health. There is no better reward.

Re-examine the perspective you have on the challenges you face as well as those of your friends and family and community. See how easily preventable many of them are when you deal with things before they exist and when you refuse to be attached to the ideas that are responsible for your problems.

There are three steps to enlightenment that people typically pass through:

1. The first way is through suffering. This is when you have big problems that cause you long periods of misery. The reason you had these long stretches of misery is because you treasure what is difficult to realize. You eventually come to a place where you can reflect on those huge obstacles (such as death, addiction, fina - cial loss, divorce, betrayal, illness) and see in retrospect that they were gifts disguised as problems.

2. The second is by being in the present moment. You are dancing with enlightenment when a crisis erupts and you are able to ask yourself; *what do I have to learn from this experience right now? What gift is hidden in this misfortune? Or what is this situation trying to tell me?* This is where you experience a quiet calm and resolve that is all knowing and powerful. This is when you begin to become at one with all that is.

3. The third is by seeing big problems coming and getting

out in front of them in advance. This means that you act before the difficulties occur or that you sense disorder coming your way and manage it all before it erupts. Here you are the observer who is completely in tune with the universal fl ws of nature. You anticipate an argument, play it out in your mind quickly and then are able to neutralize the negative energy because you got ahead of it. You have become harmonized by not acting in your old problem-producing ways. Enlightened people prevent difficulties rather than solve them. And it becomes easier the more you do it.

Buddhism

The other philosophy that kept popping up while writing this book is Buddhism. Let's have a quick review of this philosophy.

Buddhism teaches that the middle way is between self-denial and self-indulgence. This is the path to reach enlightenment. Buddhism teaches that if people live in a moderate way, just like the Buddha did when he lived the middle way, this inequality will be reduced and the problems can be avoided. This Middle Eastern philosophy has four noble truths:

- First, dissatisfaction and suffering exist and are universally experienced.

- Second, desire and attachment are the cause of dissatisfaction and suffering.

- Third, there is an end to dissatisfaction and suffering.

- Fourth, the end can be attained by journeying on the noble eightfold path.

The eightfold path of the Buddha is:

1. Right view - Understanding the four noble truths, see things as they truly are without delusions or distortions for all things change, develop wisdom by knowing how things work, knowing oneself and others.

2. Right thinking – Decide to set life on a correct path. Wholehearted resolution and dedication to overcoming the dislocation of self-centred craving through development of loving kindness, empathy and compassion.

3. Right speech- Abstinence from lies and deceptions, backbiting, idle babble and abusive speech. Cultivate honesty and truthfulness: practice speech that is kind and benevolent. Let your words reflect your desire to help, not harm others.

4. Right conduct – Follow the 5 precepts. – Practice selfless conduct that reflects the highest statement of the life you want to live. Express conduct that is peaceful honest and pure, showing compassion for all beings.

5. Right livelihood – Earn a living that does not harm living things. Avoid work that causes suffering to others or that makes a decent virtuous life impossible. Do not engage in any occupation that opposes or distracts one from the path. Love and serve our world through your work.

6. Right effort – Seek to make the balance between the exertion of following the spiritual path and a moderate life that is not overzealous. Work to develop more

wholesome mind states while gently striving to go deeper and live more fully.

7. Right mindfulness – Become intensely aware of all states in the body, feeling and mind. Through constant vigilance in thought, speech and action, seek to rid the mind of self-centred thoughts that separate and replace them with those that bind all being together. Be aware of your thoughts, emotion, and body in the present moment. Your thoughts create your reality and the world in which you live.

8. Right concentration – Deep meditation to lead to a higher state of consciousness (enlightenment) through the application of meditation and mental discipline to seek to extinguish the last flame of grasping consciousness and develop an emptiness that has room to embrace and love all things.

These are just the two philosophies that I checked into; two behemoth philosophies on the middle ground. I wanted to include these philosophies in this book because it reinforces that **Conquering From Within** is the only option. The abundance is only found when you have looked deep enough inside. If you find that you are not experiencing this holy grail of existence, take another look at yourself; ask yourself some hard questions. I am talking about really examining yourself, putting your perceptions and beliefs to the stress test of what you now know is the right path.

"I wanted to include these philosophies in this book because it reinforces that 'conquering from within' is the only option"

It is really up to you whether you want to behave the way of the powerful. All of the great teachings reveal the way of the centre, it all ends up at centre so be comfortable there, it is the way of balance. Constantly be looking to see if that is where you are living or if you are lost in the extremes. The extremes create their opposites, the wise avoid them. Find the balance at the centre and you will live in harmony. You are always executing some thought and action so why not make it the way of the strong, the way of the warrior. This path is easily followed, it already resides within; you just need to polish it up a bit. Refine a few people skills, tweak the daily habits, carve an attitude adjustment, a little interior cleaning and you're near the top in thinking. It is there for the taking, nobody has any more right to a life overfl wing with abundance than you.

This is where your best life lives, be sure of it. Why wouldn't you want to be at peace, focused, happy, rich, wise, a distribution centre of joy, relaxed, fulfilled, be powerful and above all be full of love? You now understand what is required to become enlightened. It is on this path that you will fina - ly get the bounty you deserve. You will become a lion not a sheep, you will become blessed and unstoppable, powerful, shoulders back, head up, light stepping, free as a bird, whistling Dixie. There are many riches and opportunities available when we think and behave in harmony with the natural laws of the universe, when there is no push or pull, just being.

"The extremes create their opposites, the wise avoid them"

Don't confuse this with passiveness or lack of presence and action because that is exactly the opposite of what these teachings and this book represent. You will become well acquainted with this powerful feeling of enlightenment and strength as it begins to surge through you. Enlightenment is the resting place of the strong. This is the pit stop where we refuel, where we "get ourselves together", where we prepare ourselves for the joy and possibilities of the future. It is here where ground zero exists and no inventory taken. It is here where you can unlock the life of your desires.

This new found balance and perspective will immediately give you the excitement to build the life you always wanted because you can see how easy it actually is. Right now you are probably thinking, "man oh man, have I ever wasted a lot of my time with all of the nonsense in my head." That's ok, everyone has. Forgive yourself, heal and move on. No one was born with an operations manual or set of instructions, we are all just doing the best we can with what we have been given. Having wasted time in the past makes zero difference right now, it's in the rear view mirror, irrelevant. From here the focus is on you, the focus is on forward.

TAKEAWAYS

- Make decisions carefully because they have a compounding effect. They multiply and create your life.

- Would you like 3.28 years of 24 hours a day to do whatever you want? You can and you know how; it's the same as winning the lottery.

- Thought habits are forces that hold the destinies of men and women. Your thoughts turn into your daily habits which become who you are.

- Your life is a result of the millions of decisions that you have made prior to this. Make sure as you move forward you decide wisely.

- Be careful not to double your workload. Always be on guard for the double workload effect. It is a momentum killer.

- The middle ground is a place of rest and reprieve from the extremes. Be careful not to spend your time on the extremes of life. The extremes can be full time projects that take up all your mental energy.

- In order to enjoy the middle ground one must first establish a quiet mind, a mind free of the incessant chatter.

- If you want to go in depth a little more with the Toa Te Ching or Buddhism I strongly suggest picking up a few books, it can change your life.

- Our energy needs to be used for enjoying life, being happy and fulfilling ourselves. Do not waste your energy in the extremes, arguing, being unhappy, restless, experiencing negativity, with the wrong person, sad or lonely.

CHAPTER 5

INTERNAL DIALOGUE

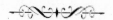

Being careful of what you tell yourself is, in my opinion, one of the most important lessons you can teach yourself. After all, you are the one who has the ability to tell yourself who you are, thus creating your characteristics and truly designing your life.

How often have you gone to bed, overcome with negative thoughts swirling in your head with regard to some event in your life? You think the same thoughts over and over, pouring over detail after detail, pondering all manner of "what-ifs," and you end up awake for hours, tossing and turning until your alarm rings early the next morning. You can hit the snooze button all you like but it won't change the fact that you wasted hours forecasting negative scenarios that have never happened and possibly never will.

This is time you will never get back, precious time and energy wasted.

Your mind twists and turns for hours instead of staying relaxed, being grateful, dreaming up possibilities, creating and conserving your energy for the morning so you can start the day fresh with vigor and vitality.

I don't know why our minds conjure up all of these negative outcomes, but they do. All of this ruminating is not just a waste of time and energy but may even serve to create an undesired outcome in the end. There is a simple premise in life that must be mastered: where the mind goes, the energy fl ws. Whatever you think about will draw on your resources and the laws of the universe. You will attract that which you think most about. You need to be super careful what you think about and which thoughts you cling to and make into reality.

"You will attract that which you think most about"

Time is a commodity just like anything else and perhaps the most important one, so don't waste it. Don't stay up all night with your mind going around in circles. Sometimes you'll fall asleep only to wake up frightened and disoriented and then your mind will start spinning all over again like a skipping record. Most of us who have logged some serious time here on Earth have done this. We have wasted days, weeks, even years going to bed with the same negative thoughts, woke up with the same negative thoughts, carried the thoughts with us all day and went to sleep with the same thoughts running wild in our head and then woke up the next day to do it all over again.

Instead, tell yourself all the things you are grateful for. Conjure up all the good things about yourself to keep the negative thoughts out. After all, we don't want to let our brains become overwhelmed and suffocated by negativity. Once that rabbit hole opens, it is not easily closed; it can lead to real problems that take a long time to solve. So start now by cutting out negative thoughts by whatever method works best for you and your lifestyle.

Meditate, do yoga, take long quiet walks in nature, listen to the birds, go for a run, read a book, whatever it takes. For me, the negative thoughts still enter if we're being honest here, those thoughts can't ever be eliminated 100 percent, but they just don't stay for long anymore. When I first started meditating, I wasn't able to stop the unwanted thoughts. The goal isn't to stop them, it is to slow them down and observe them as they go by. It took weeks of practice until I got to the point where, eventually, I was able to slow them down and in some cases have literal moments of nothingness.

You are ready to grow when you finally realize that the voice inside or the "I" who is always talking will never be fulfilled. It always has a problem with something. Ask yourself this question, when was the last time you had nothing bothering you? Before you had the problems you have now there were problems before that, just different ones. And you will realize that once this one is gone another one will be around the corner. In the end you will never be free of problems until you are free from the part within that has so many problems. When you run into a problem that is disturbing you, don't ask, "what should I do about it?" instead ask, "what part of me is being disturbed by this?" If you tell yourself there is a problem, you already believe there is a problem outside that needs your attention.

We get to choose what we think. I prefer to spend my time on this earth thinking positively about ideas big, small and in between and other things that truly matter to me. Why would you want to tell yourself things that will make you feel bad? It makes no sense, yet it seems to be human nature.

Place an elastic band around your wrist, just a small one with some good snap to it. When you have a negative thought or tell yourself something that isn't true, snap the elastic band on your wrist. It won't hurt but it will bring you back to where your mind belongs. It is a gentle reminder, or not so gentle, depending on your pain tolerance that your thoughts should focus on the miracle you are; how much love you have for yourself, how fortunate you are to be alive, how much your family loves you and how fortunate you are to be simply be you. It will snap you back to the reality of how blessed you truly are to be on the beautiful ride of life.

This is true for all of us. We have been given exactly what we need to be our authentic true selves. When you tell yourself you aren't pretty enough, athletic enough, big enough, skinny enough, rich enough, whatever you're telling yourself, you are lying to yourself. People lie to themselves all the time, it is a common human practice. It's a way to subconsciously justify and accept mediocrity, thus avoiding what you know you should be doing, which is putting a solid plan together around what you want followed by developing your daily habits around what you want, and then waking up at 5 am every day for years to get it.

As humans, we love the easy path, the path of least resistance, the known. This way of living is so much easier than getting out of your comfort zone and taking risks. However, out of your comfort zone is where the magic in life lies. It lies in the abyss of uncertainty and the uncomfortable. We have all heard a thousand times that it is the man or woman who pushes him or herself to the limit, who fails time and time again yet keeps going, who are revered and honoured in some special way. No matter who we're talking about, I can guarantee you they did not do it for public accolades or recognition. They did it because there was a fire bu ning inside of them.

Mediocrity, on the flip side, is easy to achieve. In fact, you really don't have to do much to be mediocre. It is, essentially, our default position. If you find a job that simply pays your bills, have a spouse or lover that you are not passionate about, have friends who are ambitiously average, or watch TV until all hours of the night only to get out of bed in the morning with little passion or excitement, then you're well on your way to membership in Club Mediocre.

I encourage you to slow your mind. You don't need anything more or anyone else in order to be grateful. When you show gratitude, you feel good, and this fl w of good energy can carry you through the day. Gratitude instantly opens up your mind and allows the multiplication of positive thoughts and feelings. The softening and opening of your heart will give rise to more love and fl w. There is a direct correlation. These are often described as vibrations. Our thoughts influence our vibrations. Our vibrations are what we put out into the world, to the people around us. The mind tells itself how it feels and the body then follows with a vibrational state of being. Be kind to yourself. You just showed up here on Earth and, if you're like most of us, you're simply trying your best with no real road map or how-to guide. Most of us have been given a decent upbringing with reasonable teachings from our parents. Many of us, however, haven't been given much direction and guidance. Take it easy on yourself, no matter the background you come from, and don't think yourself to death.

The mind is a computer and most of the time we are simply replaying all of the daily negative rubbish that we have seen in life, on TV and have experienced since we were children. The time has come to end the incessant internal dialogue of the negative mind. It is time to change your negative thoughts and get back on track to being who you really can be.

It is time to stop the negative thoughts about your boss, your spouse, your kids, your hair, your car, your weight, your lot in life and everything else you tell yourself that is negative. Quit cold turkey, just don't do it anymore. Once the negative thoughtfl w is replaced with new thoughts, you will be amazed at what opens up to you. The world becomes the magical place you were once told it would be and, really, is supposed to be.

To get to the place of true inner freedom, you must be able to objectively listen to your problems and not get lost in them. You cannot and will not be able to find a solution if you are lost in the energy of your problem. You must break the habit of thinking that the solution to your problems is to rearrange outside things. The only solution is to go inside and release the part of you that has so many problems with reality. Once you can do this, you will see what remains and will be easily able to handle it.

Here is a question: What would you think if someone started to talk to you the way you talk to yourself inside? Speaks whatever they think, questions you all the time, tells you that you "can't do it", calls you names and just generally isn't happy with you? After a while you would tell them to shut up and never come back. Isn't it strange how you never tell your inner voice to stop or tell it to leave? It makes no difference how much trouble it causes, you will listen and be there. It is only after you have looked deep inside that you will see there is only one problem and that problem is you. You have been causing every problem that you have ever had. You really have to want to get rid of this before it will go. You will eventually realize that you have to distance yourself from your psyche. Understand the situation you are in and realize that your soul is more powerful than your mind.

"The only way to change how you feel is to change how you think"

You have everything you need right now and you are perfect exactly the way you are. You just need to change your internal dialogue so you can truly realize not only how great you are in this moment but also how great you can become. Change the internal dialogue, change the things you tell yourself and change your life. Don't spend another moment wasting the energy you have been given. The only way to change how you feel is to change how you think.

The underlying emotion behind our negative thoughts is fear. We fear the unknown. We fear our perceived lack of strength. We fear that we have no idea of the outcome. We become so afraid to do anything because we worry about what might happen; we can become paralyzed by it.

Our insecurities cause us to talk ourselves out of the very thing we want the most, because we are afraid. Many fears are just excuses to maintain the status quo - self-designed fears to permit us to remain mediocre and not challenge ourselves. When we are afraid of something, we avoid it.

"You must attack your insecurities and fears by letting them out, in order to conquer them"

People who are afraid of heights avoid any activity above ground level, no matter what it is without considering if such a fear can be overcome, or without wondering if the benefits of the activity outweigh the risks. You must attack your insecurities and fears while letting them out, in order to conquer them.

The excuse of fear allows oneself to justify the lack of trying and effort. Remember, most of us are comfortable with the easiest path, and having the excuse of fear in our back pocket allows us to stay caged and is used to justify our life of no challenge. Just as it is easy to blame your circumstances on someone and something else, it is as easy to let yourself and your friends know that you're simply afraid. Don't be afraid, have a champion mindset. Challenge your fears and they will no longer be fears. The inertia and the momentum you get from tackling your fears will be enormous and fulfilling, and it will snowball to your amazement.

Our best life is not found inside the mundane activities of life. We need to stretch ourselves because getting outside of our comfort zone is important. See where it takes you. People of substance and achievement have had to stretch themselves outside of their comfort zone in order to find their true love, passion and meaning, and the same is true for all of us.

Fear of the unknown is the primary reason why many people don't end up living life on their terms. They're afraid to lose. Well, guess what? You've already lost if you don't try.

Be a champion. Get out there and make some mistakes, screw things up and, in the process, learn new ways of doing things. That growth will be the barometer against which you can measure yourself, and tell whether or not you are on the right track. The internal feedback along the way is the guide for your life. What your emotions are, or what you feel, need to be the compass of your life. A simple shift in thinking can make a huge difference.

"Men often become what they believe themselves to be"

You see, it is all in what we tell ourselves and what we think about. If we think we are tired, then we'll feel tired; if we think we are lacking, then we are; if we think we are poor, we will be; if we think we can't do something then guess what, we can't. Just as Mahatma Gandhi said, "men often become what they believe themselves to be. If I believe I cannot do something, it makes me incapable of doing it. But when I believe I can, then I acquire the ability to do it even if I didn't have it in the beginning."

If you say to yourself each day that you don't like your job, aren't satisfie with your income, your love life, your friends, where you live or how you feel, then I encourage you to take a critical look at your thinking. Don't lie to yourself about your circumstances, be clear on where you are today. Just don't let your circumstances define you and dictate where you go from here. Where you go from here is the most important factor in self-development. How you shape your character is, as you know, very important to the forward journey.

One of the more desirable characteristics in someone is charisma. Not many things feel better than being around someone who is charismatic. There is just an energy field around them that is on a little bit higher frequency than everyone else. To that end, I wanted to unearth this quality to give you some insight into how you too can become charismatic.

Charisma can be learned much like anything else and has tremendous influence in all aspects of your life. If you spend enough time thinking and acting charismatically, you will soon become more charismatic. You can be an extrovert or an introvert, it makes no difference, but you are going to need a little bit of charisma to get where you are going. Contrary to popular belief, people are not simply born charismatic, innately magnetic from birth. If charisma was an inherent attribute, charismatic people would always be captivating and that's just not the case.

Even for the most engaging superstar, they can turn on and off their charisma like flipping a switch. They can go from completely unnoticed to flipping the switch of charisma simply by changing body language. Research in recent years has shown that charisma is the result of non-specific non-verbal behaviours; it is not an inherent or magical quality. The average person with a little bit of charisma immediately becomes more engaging and falls into more opportunities.

Charisma can be broken down into three core elements: presence, power and warmth. These elements deepen our conscious behaviours as well as other factors we don't consciously control. People pick up on small changes in our body's energies and signals that we don't even know we are sending. We need to take a look at body language and how our signals can be influenced.

Through charisma training you will learn how to how to adopt a charismatic posture, how to warm-up your eye contact, and how to modulate your voice in a way that makes people pay attention. Three quick tips to gain an instant charisma boost in conversation: First, lower the intonation of your voice at the end of your sentences. Second, reduce how quickly and often you nod. Third, pause for a full two seconds before you speak. The most charismatic people you will meet will do one thing better than anything else and that is simply listen to the other person with connected eyes and really genuinely care about what the other person is saying. This is the foundation of charisma.

If you are able to perform this one act, you are charismatic. We understand that proficiency at singing, playing chess, playing the piano or shooting a puck requires conscious practice. Charisma is a skill that can also be developed through conscious practice and because we are interacting with people all the time, we get to use and develop our charisma tools on a daily basis.

People pick up on messages that we often don't realize

we're sending through small changes in our body language. In order to be charismatic, we need to choose mental states that make our body language, words, and behaviours fl w together and express three core elements of charisma.

Presence is the foundation for everything so let's start there. Our presence is all we have. We may have a car, a boat and a house but presence is everything we have and are. Make sure you have good presence.

"Make sure you are fully attentive"

What this means is make sure you are in the moment when you are around other people, make sure you are fully attentive. Don't be half there with your eyes glancing over their shoulder at the person walking behind them or don't let your mind wander. People can read facial expressions in as little as seventeen milliseconds. If you are not mentally with someone in a conversation they will know immediately. You've surely had the experience of talking to someone who wasn't really listening, where they were just going through the motions of listening preparing their next sentence before you even fi - ished speaking. How did you feel then? Brushed off, less than, resentful, annoyed? Not only can the lack of presence be visible, it can also be perceived as disingenuous, resulting in even worse emotional consequences.

"The ability to be fully present makes you stand out from the crowd; it makes you memorable"

When you are perceived as disingenuous, it is impossible

119

to generate rapport, trust or loyalty. If you don't have these things then you don't have and can't have charisma. You want to be present with people as it will build your confide ce and charisma, opening the door to deeper relationships and more opportunities. Even a minor increase in your capacity for presence can have a major effect on those around you. Very few of us are ever fully present. Imagine the impact you can have on your environment if you are fully present. The next time you are in a conversation check whether you are fully engaged or your mind is wandering.

The ability to be fully present makes you stand out from the crowd; it makes you memorable. When you are fully present, even a fi e minute conversation with someone can leave them saying "wow" and make you feel emotionally connected.

Your presence aligns others with your beauty, when you have heightened awareness, you see beauty everywhere and in everything because you're emitting the quality of beauty. At this higher energy called enlightenment you see beauty in everything, in everyone, young or old, rich or poor, light or dark, with no distinctions. Everything is perceived from a perspective of appreciation rather than judgement. As you carry this feeling of beauty appreciation to the presence of others, people are inclined to see themselves as you see them. Your awareness of beauty shines through you and impacts others in a way that causes them to see beauty in the same way. This is the ripple effect a rock has when thrown in the water. People begin to feel appealing and better about themselves as they circulate the high energy of beauty. Be a circulator of beauty because when people feel beautiful they act in beautiful ways.

The people that you are with feel like they have your full attention and that they are the most important person in the world at that moment. What an amazing gift that is to be able to make someone feel like they are valued and respected. Once you begin to distribute this love to people in your life, the ripple effect takes over and soon your world is awash in abundance.

Meditation teacher Stephanie Holden has made the practice of "being present" a lifetime study. Here is what she says, "In most moments we have continuous internal commentary on what is happening and what we should do next. We might greet a friend with a hug, but the warmth of our greeting becomes blurred by our computations about how long to embrace or what we're going to say when we are done. We rush through the motions, not being fully present." Being present enables you to fully notice and drink in the good moments. Remember that, every time you bring yourself back to full presence you reap great rewards; you become more impactful, more memorable and come across as more grounded. You are laying the foundation for a charismatic presence.

Being seen as powerful means being perceived as able to affect the world around us in various ways: through influence on or authority over others, with large amounts of money, expertise, intelligence, sheer physical strength or high social status. We look for clues of power in someone's appearance, other's reaction to this person, and, most of all, in the person's body language.

Warmth, simply put, is goodwill towards others. Warmth tells us whether or not people will want to use whatever power they have in our favour. Being seen as warm means being perceived as any of the following: caring, benevolent, altruistic, compassionate, empathetic or just willing to impact the world in a positive way. Warmth is assessed almost entirely though body language and behaviour. A deeper relationship with the world and the people in it requires this layer of warmth. You will know it when you have it because you will, without effort, become curious about people and their lives. Life will become less about you.

To have charismatic **power** is to have an ability to see yourself in others. It is an ability to relate yourself to others whereby everyone feels as one. It is the ability to make two people much stronger than one person; three people stronger than two etc. A powerfully charismatic person doesn't always lead but can be the glue that keeps a group strong. When you see a charismatically powerful person you will notice a certain confidence and belie   in themselves and others.

"Warmth, simply put, is goodwill towards others"

How do we gauge power and warmth? Imagine that you're meeting someone for the first time. In most instances, you don't have the benefit of a background check, earlier interviews, job history, or even the time to wait and see their behaviour. So in most instances you have to make a quick guess. Throughout our daily interactions, we instinctively look for clues with which to evaluate warmth or power and then we adjust our assumptions accordingly.

Expensive clothes leads us to *assume* wealth, friendly body language leads us to *assume* good intentions, nice big smile leads us to *assume* happiness, a confident posture leads us to *assume* the person has something to be confident about. In essence, people will tend to accept whatever you project. Just by increasing your projection of power or projection of warmth, you increase your level of charisma. When you can project power and warmth together, you have maximized your charismatic potential.

The next time you are out and about shopping or just

walking around, start talking to a stranger, gather their eye contact and see if you can distribute your warmth to them through your body language and eye contact. You will be able to tell as the warmth will reciprocate straight back to you from them.

Projecting presence, power and warmth through your body language is often all you need to be perceived as charismatic. This comes with a challenge. There is far too much body language for us to control consciously and our body language expresses our mental state whether we like it or not. Our facial expressions, posture, voice, and all other elements of body language reflect our true mental and emotional condition every second. Because we don't control this fl w consciously, whatever we have in our head will show up in our body language. Like a lighthouse, your light comes from within.

We can't micromanage charismatic body language. Charismatic behaviours must start in your mind. If your internal state is not charismatic, no amount of effort and will power can make up for it. Sooner or later some of your underlying thoughts and feelings will show through. On the other hand, if your internal state is fulfilled, happy, content and charismatic, then the right body language will come forth effortlessly? Put some time into your charisma, this particular trait will carry you great distances.

Remember: you get to decide, you are the designer of your life. You get to pick who your friends are, what you listen to, where and who you work, where you live, what car you drive and any number of other decisions, both big and small. Be courageous and make some changes to your thinking. Things can only improve. What would be the worst possible outcome if you were to make the changes required to live the life you want?

When we ask ourselves this question – "what's the worst

than can happen?" we tend to spin into some out-of-control thoughts. What if I'm homeless, have no money, no friends, lose my job, or my significa t other leaves me? Blah, blah, blah. This is most common when extracting yourself from a long term relationship or considering quitting a job and jumping into the unknown. Chances are that's not going to happen and you are letting the unknown cripple you. This is the kiss of death. Embrace the unknown as a long-time friend that you look forward to seeing again. The future holds no fear but the fear you create in your mind. You need to change your thought patterns of the future and look at it in a different light.

"You get to decide, you are the designer of your life"

James Allen writes brilliantly, in his book *As A Man Thinketh,* about the fact that you literally are what you think. He says that you either make or unmake yourself. "By your armory of thoughts, you forge the weapons with which you destroy yourself or you fashion the tools with which you build a life of joy, strength and peace."[1]

Allen goes on further to explain that, by carefully choosing our thoughts, we can reach close to perfection in life. But if we are abusive with our choices and reckless in our thoughts, we will "descend to the level of a mere animal."[2] Allen believes, as I do, that we are the masters of our thoughts and that, through them, we can determine our destiny. Allen writes about our minds as analogous to a garden and suggests that how we

---

1   Allen, James, *As A Man Thinketh* (New York: JP Tarcher/Penguin, 2008).

2   Ibid.

tend to it affects its production. He says that by "weeding" out wrong thoughts and "cultivating" right and pure thoughts you can create outer conditions of your life that are as harmonious as your inner state.

Allen reassures us that every stage we are at in life has its purpose, and we are in the perfect positions to learn and grow. He warns against feeling victimized by circumstances and advises that we see ourselves as creative powers in charge of our own development instead. He says it is only when we reach maturity and take responsibility for our condition that we will progress and discover all of our hidden powers as well as the possibilities that lie within us.

According to Allen, thoughts of fear, doubt, indecision, lazy and impure thoughts, hateful and condemnatory thoughts, as well as selfish thoughts lead us to undesirable states. Beautiful, pure, courageous, gentle, loving and forgiving thoughts, on the other hand, will lead us to uplifting and preservative circumstances of peace, freedom, abundance, prosperity and success.

Calmness of mind is one of the beautiful jewels of wisdom. It is the result of long and patient effort in self-control. Its presence is an indication of ripened experience, and of a more than ordinary knowledge of the laws and operations of thought.

A person becomes calm in the measure that one understands themselves as a thought evolved being. Such knowledge necessitates the understanding of others as the result of thought, and as one develops a right understanding, and sees more and more clearly the internal relations of things by the action of cause and effect, one ceases to fuss and fume and worry and grieve, and remains poised, steadfast, serene.

The calm person, having learned how to govern themselves, knows how to adapt themselves to others; and they, in turn, revere others' spiritual strength, and feel that they can learn from them and rely upon them. The more tranquil a person becomes, the greater is their success, their influenc , their power for good. Even the ordinary trader will find their business prosperity increase as one develops a greater self-control and equanimity, for people will always prefer to deal with a person whose demeanor is strongly equable.

The strong, calm person is always loved and revered. They are like a shade-giving tree in a thirsty land, or a sheltering rock in a storm. Who does not love a tranquil heart, a sweet-tempered, balanced life? It does not matter whether it rains or shines, or what changes come to those possessing these blessings, for they are always sweet, serene, and calm.

That exquisite poise of character which we call serenity is the last lesson of culture; it is the fl wering of life, the fruitage of the soul. It is as precious as wisdom, more to be desired than gold. How insignificant mere money seeking looks in comparison with a serene life, a life that dwells in the ocean of truth, beneath the waves, beyond the reach of tempests, in the eternal calm!

How many people do we know who sour their lives, who ruin all that is sweet and beautiful by explosive tempers, who destroy their poise of character, and make bad blood? It is a question of whether the great majority of people do or do not ruin their lives and mar their happiness by lack of self-control. Few people we meet in life are well-balanced and have the exquisite poise which is characteristic of the finished person

Yes, humanity surges with uncontrolled passion, is tumultuous with ungoverned grief, is blown about by anxiety and doubt. Only the wise man, only he whose thoughts are controlled and purified, makes the winds and the storms of the soul obey him".

Flip the negative thoughts into positive ones and tell yourself how your life will look when you execute your new thoughts. Do not stay a slave to what happened yesterday. When you change the way you think, you will change your reality. You can have more satisfaction in your monetary endeavours, you won't have to deal with "those people" at work, you can stretch your creative mind, improve your friendships, and you can have more freedom and more love.

If you escape the fear in your mind, you can reach the mountaintop. Every person who has stretched their beliefs and let go of fear has found that life is more rewarding and fulfil - ing. I think we can all agree on this. These people are far and few between.

If you are like most people, you will have an internal desire for more. You see, as humans we are designed to expand and grow. We are designed to want more, attract more, achieve more, have more, love more, laugh more, give more, etc. This is in us at our DNA level. Every person I have ever met is always striving for more. Once they get somewhere or reach a goal, they immediately set another.

"If you escape the fear in your mind, you can reach the mountaintop"

We must work at life. It isn't something we were given to just coast through. If you choose to coast, I can assure you that you will not reap the benefits that life has to offer. Like the fl w of water, it will dump you out at its lowest point. Life is meant to be massively fulfillin . The difference is some people will work for it and others won't.

Be one of the people who works for life and all it has to

offer. When you put in a little bit of effort, you will be amazed at the results. You received the same God-given talents that the person beside you received. The truth is that some of the people who reach the highest and achieve the most in life are the ones that were given less talent than you. They just worked hard, failed sometimes and grew into who they are today. They didn't tell themselves that they couldn't do it.

The man who climbed Mount Kilimanjaro with no legs didn't say, "I can't climb this mountain." The 65 year old lady who swam from Florida to Cuba didn't tell herself that she couldn't do it. They told themselves it could be done. They weren't sure how many times they would fail, but they told themselves they would do it nonetheless.

When you go to bed at night, remind yourself that you were created as an equal to the next person. In fact, you probably have more talent and gifts than the next person, so use it accordingly, don't waste it. Remind yourself of the miracle that you are. Other people would sacrifice greatly to have your abilities and talents and live your life. The universe loves and rewards people who work hard, fail, get hurt, get back up again to do it all over again until it's done. This is also very personally rewarding and translates into more success down the road. Success breeds success. When we win, we feel great and there is usually a natural desire to do it again in order to create the same positive feelings.

It is almost like Pavlov's dog, if I could equate it to that. Dopamine is released into the brain when we feel good, so when we win, we keep going back for more. This is why desire is such a force of human nature.

People with a victim mentality often let failures take them down. I'm sure you know people like this. Friends, family, neighbours and community members you know who feel they have been wronged and are bitter. They believe they can't get ahead because of some set of circumstances that will forever serve as an obstacle. It's like crabs in a bucket. Once you put a second crab in a bucket and the first one tries to escape, the second one will pull it right back down.

Thinking about yourself as a positive person and focusing on your positive attributes are critical components to how you will feel. How you feel every day is a direct function of what you tell yourself about yourself. I'm not advocating being disillusioned, if you're behaving badly or just generally feeling miserable, you're going to need to take some active steps to get back on track. If you are like most of us, you are an active and contributing member of society, have friends, make good decisions and stay out of trouble. If this is the case, go easy on yourself.

"How you feel every day is a direct function of what you tell yourself about yourself"

The best part is you get to tell yourself who you are. Tell yourself the right things. Tell yourself that you are a champion, a warrior, one who doesn't quit despite the circumstances. Talk highly of people and don't gossip. Dwell on the positive and not negative events from the past. Yesterday is who you "were". This moment, and all the upcoming future moments is who you "are" and "will be." Don't be defined y your past. So, you made a mistake last week? So what? Don't do it again. Recreate who you are. You can't change your past but you can shape your future. It is okay to make a mistake but if you make the same mistake twice, this is no longer a mistake but a decision. There's a three step approach to letting go of the past and expecting good in the future:

Number one: It is what it is, accept it. It doesn't matter what has happened in your life. Some of you have had disturbing things happen in your past. These things may have really affected your life. Either you are going to control it, or it is going to control you. It is what it is, accept it.

Number two: Harvest the good. There is good in everything and the more you look for it, the more you will find. Harvest the good.

Number three: Forgive all the rest. Forgive means to let go of it completely. Abandon. Just let it go. Quit dwelling on what is wrong. Stop thinking about all of the negative things or people in your life. You are blowing these out of proportion. Forgive it all.

It is a very common human condition to dwell on the negative things in life or to worry about the unknown. We dwell on what someone said about us yesterday, the idiot who cut you off in traffic (yes, admit it, you're still thinking about it), the person who wronged us, the lack of whatever it is you think you deserve. You get the point, always dwelling on negative things, always worrying.

When acknowledged as a sign of change, worry is transitory and is simply part of the world changing. If you are able to view your life from the viewpoint of the infinite observer, stress, anxiety and concerns blend into the eternal mix. From this perspective, picture how the things you feel depressed about now will feel in ten, a hundred, a thousand, and a million years from now. Rearrange your thoughts about who you are. Cultivating an awareness of the infinite aspect of yourself is the way to tap into the limitless source of creativity that fl ws through you.

Why do negative emotions and negative self-talk in our heads become what often control us? This conditioning certainly starts with our families, teachers, friends and our up-bringing. Really look at your parents the next time you see them. Are they excited, are they adventurous, do they have passion about life, how do they speak, what words do they choose, are they negative or positive? This will be your insight, a true look, into the beginnings of who you are.

Negative emotions have a bigger impact and lasting impression because we are conditioned to be this way by our environment. Next time you turn on the TV, listen to all the death, rape, destruction, murder and general chaos as you flip from channel to channel. It will startle you once you start really paying attention. The next time the music stops on the radio station you're listening to, and the news comes on, you will hear the same negativity.

There are 8 billion people in the world. You would be amazed if I told you that .000001 percent of all the people cause all the world's problems. These few people commit all the murders, the rapes, the explosions, thievery and the chaos. That means that there are almost 99.99999% of the population doing normal or great things every day. We only hear about the very small minority who make poor choices and cause problems. Here is the completely bizarre part: the actions of this miniscule percentage of the population are what is covered on TV news 95 percent of the time. People like chaos, it makes them feel better about their lives, and the news stations know it.

Remember, TV stations make their money from sponsors or companies who buy time to advertise their products. TV stations examine very closely what gets the highest ratings. They know that people prefer to watch chaos and bedlam over anything else, so this is what they put all over the television news.

If you want to be happy, you must remove negativity in

your life. You can't be happy and sad at the same time. You must remove the negativity otherwise it will always be there. Stop watching the news and turn off the car radio when the news comes on. This one single move will stop a tremendous fl w of negativity. Completely remove yourself from all the negative people in your life. Yes you will have to make a few hard decisions but your happiness is more important than your energy sucking friend or family member.

"If you want to be happy, you must remove negativity in your life"

Stop allowing negative people to influence you. You can see the energy vampires a mile away, they are easy to spot. You can see it in their eyes, see it in their posture, hear it in their words and feel it in their energy. Do yourself a favour and stay away from these people. Do not give them any of your energy because this is all they want. They need your energy to give life to their energy, regardless of how negative it is. You can't be a negative person if no one is around and there is no one to speak to, this is why they try to suck you into their world. They need you to fuel their negativism.

Your energy isn't for sale, so don't let them have it. Negative people want to suck you down into their sad abyss and steal the mental space in your head. They want to steal your valuable limited time on earth. It is not meant to be given away so cheaply and easily. Reserve the right to say "no" to these people and on your own terms.

So we have two huge reasons, so far, as to why we stay up in bed at night going over the negative thoughts in our minds. Bad things have a better chance of happening when you are going over all of the negative thoughts of the day while you should be sleeping. Take some time to reflect on negativity from the day, but spend very little time on it. Recognize it, tell yourself how you will do it differently next time and then let it go.

"Being grateful opens a portal for more beautiful things to enter your life"

Spend most of your time on the positive, the things you did right, the people you love, the opportunities that are before you and the wonderful moments you had during that day. Gratitude is the easiest way to bring yourself to the proper state of mind. If you are grateful for all that you have in your life, then you cannot help but feel good. If you are stewing about all of the negative things, then you can't help but feel sad and depressed.

Being grateful opens a portal for more beautiful things to enter your life. I think we can agree that it is difficult for beautiful and great things to enter your life if you are grumpy, angry, sad and downtrodden. You couldn't see the beautiful and great things if they hit you over the head with a hammer. You will be too mired in your negativity and your victim mentality to see the beauty before you. To allow all of the things you want into your life, simply start by being grateful. Be grateful for your life, your eyes, your arms, your breath, your family, and your job (even though you may dislike aspects of it).

Let's cut out the ridiculous sensationalism news, let's turn off the radio, and let's get rid of the negative chatter in our minds. Let's make the words that fl w from your mouth pleasant, joyful and positive. I'm speaking of an authentic ability to genuinely speak both positive and uplifting words. People always ask how you're doing in passing. Instead of saying, "getting by" or "okay" or "same ole", try "fantastic" or "living the dream", or "wonderful". These words will actually make you feel better. Try it the next time someone asks how you are doing and see how it feels. **Part of being peaceful and content is believing that you are actually doing well.**

Once you "fli " this around to the positive side, you will see your life and the opportunities in it multiply exponentially.

We have been bombarded with media since we were young children. The fl w of negativity started in our formative years and it hasn't stopped, only ramped up. It is enormous. It starts in the morning and doesn't stop all day. It is everywhere. And with the onset of social media, the fl w of negativity is absolutely relentless. Every day, all day, we are hammered with the same message. Death is everywhere, destruction is rampant, the economy is no good, and struggle is the way of life…blah, blah, blah.

But no, it isn't actually that way. Ask the people around you who are successful and happy. They will tell you a different story. **They will tell you stories of abundance, happiness, joy, adventure and being fulfilled.**

As in the words of author Thomas Troward:

"To realize the true nature of affi mative power is to possess the key to the great secret. We feel its presence in all the innumerable forms of life by which we are surrounded and we feel it as the life in ourselves; and at last someday the truth bursts upon us like a revelation that we can wield this power, this life, by the process of thought. And as soon as we see this, the importance of regulating our thinking begins to dawn upon us. We ask ourselves what this thought process is, and we then find that it is thinking affi mative force into forms which are the product of our own thought. We mentally conceive the form and then think life into it.

This must always be the nature of the creative process on whatever scale, whether on the grand scale of the Universal Cosmic Mind or on the miniature scale of the individual mind; the difference is only in degree and not in kind. It is the result of that inner mental state which, for want of a better word, we may call our emotional conception of ourselves. It is the "self" which we *feel* ourselves to be which takes forms of our own creating. For this reason, our thought must be so grounded upon knowledge that we shall feel the truth of it, and thus be able to produce in ourselves that mental attitude of feeling which corresponds to the condition which we desire to externalise.

We cannot think into manifestation a different sort of life to that which we realise in ourselves. As Horace says, "*Nemo dat quod non habet*," we cannot give what we have not got. And, on the other hand, we can never cease creating forms of some sort by our mental activity, thinking life into them. This point must be very carefully noted.

We cannot sit still producing nothing: the mental machinery *will* keep on turning out work of some sort, and it rests with us to determine of what sort it shall be. In our entire ignorance or imperfect realisation of this, we create negative forms and think life into them. We create forms of death, sickness, sorrow, trouble, and limitation of all sorts, and then think life into these forms, with the result that, however non-existent in themselves, to us they become realities and throw their shadow across the path which would otherwise be bright with the many-coloured beauties of innumerable fl wers and the glory of the sunshine.

This need not be. It is giving to the negative an affi mative force which does not belong to it. Consider what is meant by the negative. It is the absence of something. It is not-being, and is the absence of all that constitutes being. Left to itself, it remains in its own nothingness, and it only assumes form and activity when we give these to it by our thought.

Here, then, is the great reason for practising control over our thought. It is the one and only instrument we have to work with, but it is an instrument which works with the greatest certainty, for limitation if we think limitation, for enlargement if we think enlargement. Our thought as feeling is the magnet which draws to us those conditions which accurately correspond to itself. This is the meaning of the saying that "thoughts are things."

But, you say, how can I think differently from the circumstances? Certainly you are not required to say that the circumstances *at the present moment* are what they are not; to say so would be untrue; but what is wanted is not to think from the standpoint of circumstances at all. Think from that interior standpoint where there are no circumstances, and from whence you can dictate what circumstances shall be, and then leave the circumstances to take care of themselves.

Do not think of this, that, or the other particular *circumstances* of health, peace, etc., but of health, peace, and prosperity themselves. Here is an advertisement from *Pearson's Weekly*: "Think money. Big money-makers *think* money." This is a perfectly sound statement of the power of thought, although it is only an advertisement; but we may make an advance beyond thinking "money." We can think "Life" in all its fullness, together with that perfect harmony of conditions which includes all that we need of money and a thousand other good things besides, for some of which money stands as the symbol of exchangeable value, while others cannot be estimated by so material a standard.

Therefore, think life, illumination, harmony, prosperity, happiness think the things rather than this or that condition of them. And then, by the sure operation of the Universal Law, these things will form themselves into the shapes best suited to your particular case, and will enter your life as active, living forces, which will never depart from you because you know them to be part and parcel of your own being."

Troward, T. (1921). *The hidden power: And other papers on mental science.* New York: Dodd, Mead.

TAKEAWAYS

- Thoughts can become who you are and what you choose to think about controls every step of your life. Thoughts become things.

- What we think about, we attract. There is no way around this. Angry people don't attract happy people and happy people don't attract angry people.

- You get to design "who" you are. You might as well be the greatest. You have to get up and get after it.

- We must push ourselves out of our comfort zone to reach maximum achievement. Full stop here.

- Failure is not your undertaker, it is required for your success. If you are not failing, your goals are too easy and ambitions not lofty enough.

- Failure must be seen as a stepping stone towards your goals, success and accomplishments.

- There are many perspectives on which to view an event. A shift in perception can alter the direction of one's life.

- Charisma is a great characteristic to have. Like playing the piano, it can be learned. If you want more charisma, read and study it.

- True charisma comes from a mental state of being. You can't fake charisma. Charisma can be broken down into three core elements: presence, power and warmth.

CHAPTER 6
ELEVATE YOUR LIFE –
UNLEASH YOUR GREATNESS

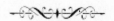

Imagine for a moment a frog living in a well. Insects get trapped in there feeding him all day, the weather never changes, always dark and moist, just perfect for a frog. It is really quite an easy life, lack of challenge just jumping from wall to wall, getting fed every day without leaving the well. This is all he knows, by all means a wonderful life to him, all needs fulfilled, the future is bright

This is until another frog hops in the well with him and tells him what he's missing. It is explained to him that there is light and sunshine outside the well and that, if you sit in the sunshine, you become a cool color that entices all the other frogs. He goes on to learn that there are lily pads that can be jumped on one after the other in a game like scenario. There are lakes and a plethora of other insects, a virtual smorgasbord outside the well.

If you eat enough food, you become large and power-ful, which also serves as an aphrodisiac to the lady frogs. He doesn't believe it. He says, "no chance, I am staying in the well" and this is comfortable and quite frankly easy. I don't believe you anyways, new buddy frog, I'm going to pass on leaving the well. I'm just too comfortable and it's too easy in here." "Ok," says new buddy frog, "all the best, enjoy the moist dark well."

Years go by and another frog jumps into the well and says exactly the same thing as the first frog. "We've got lily pads and lakes and sunshine, loads of different foods and lots of lady frogs but you have to come out of the well and out of where you are comfortable in order to find and see what this looks like." The well frog finally says, "what the hell, I have been in here for four years, locked in my own little world, and I am going to give this a chance; what is there to lose? I can always jump back in if needed."

The second frog leads the well frog to the top of the algae-filled lid of the deep cylinder. The well frog reaches his long webbed fin ers over the top of the well and immediately sees grass and sunlight. "What are those?" he asks. "That is the sun and that is grass and those over there are horses, those are cows and that hot yellow orb in the sky is designed to keep us warm out of the well. It is so precise that it circles around the Earth and keeps us warm without fail. The grass grows without effort, the stars line up in their accustom positions each night, the orb rises and falls with exact precision, everything works in perfect unison." The well frog is in complete shock as to what is available to him outside of the well. He is truly amazed.

"You will never know what is going on in the world if you choose to let the weakest parts of your life control your life"

It takes him sometime to adapt but in no time he is jumping from lily pad to lily pad, puts on a few pounds, changes colors and is living with a lady frog. He sings at night in chorus with all the other frogs, jumps from tree to tree, basks in the sunlight and eats like a king. All of a sudden, the well frog is no longer a trepidatious, afraid, cautious well frog. It is now a vibrant, buzzing, singing, lily pad-jumping frog that it should have been years ago. You will never know what is going on in the world if you choose to let the weakest parts of your life control your life. Remove the disturbance and the insecurities in your soul, this will free you from your mental bondage.

We shall never reach our true authentic selves if we don't get out of the well. Choice is the most powerful tool we have. Everything in your life boils down to our decisions. We exist in a field of infinite possibilities. Every choice we make shuts an exponential number of doors and, at the same time, opens an exponential number of doors. At any point, we can change the direction of our lives by a simple choice. It is all in our hands, our hearts, our minds and souls.

"Choice is the most powerful tool we have"

The number one choice a person should make to gain self-discovery and self-mastery is to test one's will and desire; test your resolve. Go inside your mind and form a game plan. Decide who you want to be and be that person all the time regardless of what happens. Believe me, you will get tested; we all get tested every day. When the tests come, it is your turn to display the new you. Do it once and you'll feel awkward, do it twice and you'll feel cool, do it three times and feel the power of the "new you". Work on yourself from the inside out, gathering and harnessing the power from within.

The second way to learn about you is to fail and lose; there are many lessons in success and loss. In fact almost every lesson can be learned within these events. Getting out of the well and your comfort zone is going to provide you with two of the best things in life. First, you will be able to experience the discomfort that is required in order to know comfort. Without knowing discomfort, you can't know comfort. Second, you will learn resilience. You will know what it's like to be tough, to have strength, to fall, to get hurt, to suffer and bounce back like nothing happened.

This new found resilience you gather from testing yourself will be the key that allows you to stop dragging around your life stories like a ball and chain. This new found courage will be the foundation of every future decision. This is how people become strong and confident. They just keep stacking one win on top of another. This leap of faith will provide you with everything you need. Attack your fears and insecurities so that you may be released from them. Do not go through life with the mission to avoid situations or events in order to protect yourself from your fears and insecurities; attack them instead. Stare your fears directly in the face and let them know that you are not afraid. You are the one who is going to make the decisions from here on out. There is nothing to fear.

"Attack your fears and insecurities so that you may be released from them"

Don't let these opportunities pass you by, these seemingly difficult circumstances need to be viewed as opportunities, not valleys of misfortune or difficulty. Leaving the well invites loss, failure, ridicule, some people won't like you, some will. There will be ups and downs and times when the well seems like a better idea. **Retreat is not an option**, take your lumps, take your discomfort, take the incessant internal chattering, take your broken heart and forge on to your authentic self. No one

144

belongs in a dark well; you know you are busting to come out.

While trying to make your leap out of the well a graceful one remember that your job isn't to please everyone, your job isn't to cater to others, and your job isn't to give your energy away to others. Your job is to simply be you and let the cards fall where they may. Your job is to design you and let life stress-test who you choose to be. Put yourself under pressure as a diamond does. A diamond becomes a diamond only after it has been under tremendous pressure for great periods of time.

It is really easy being you if you know what you stand for. Your job is to come from love and happiness and have good intentions. If someone doesn't like that in you, they are not right for you; walk away from them. Give the universe a chance to align everything for you. Let it show you that perfect partner, that great job, that next opportunity, the next sale, that pile of money. Living in the well will get you none of these things. You are not giving the universe or anyone in it the chance to know you and see you and become comfortable with who you are. What do you expect life in the well will provide?

There is really only one choice to make and it is not about the where you live, the car you buy, the religion you choose or the career you take. People tend to burden themselves with too many choices. At the end of the day, the choice you need to make is, "do I want to be happy or do I want to be unhappy?" It is that simple. Once you have this answer, life becomes much simpler and the path more clear. Happiness only knows the right path, there is no wrong path when you are happy and fulfilled. Don't think this is out of your control because it isn't. Your circumstances don't control your happiness, other people don't control your happiness, your spouse doesn't control your happiness, and your co-worker doesn't control your happiness.

YOU are the steward of your happiness. We all desire to

be happy in so many ways. Happiness is different to each of us but we desire it all the same. This isn't a question of, "do I want to be happy only when things are going my way?" This is a question of, "do I want to be happy regardless of what is happening in my life?" This is important because it is easy to be happy when everything is going well; it is not as easy when difficul y arises. Make sure this is an unconditional answer. The highest spiritual path lies in being happy regardless if your spouse leaves you or you lose your job or the economy collapses or the other million things that can happen.

Life throws many challenges at us, no one is immune from difficult . What we can be immune from is the sadness and anger and despair that follows being hurt. If you decide to be happy for the rest of your life, you will not only be happy but you will become enlightened. You will rise above the earthly challenges and emotions that are created in difficulty; you will have an awakening of the highest order. You don't need to go to Tibet and hang out with monks for years to become happy and enlightened. You simply must make the fi m decision that you are going to be happy regardless of what happens. Making this one decision will lead you towards enlightenment.

If you want to be happy, you have to let go of the part of you that loves the drama and the resistance to things. This is the part of you that thinks there is a reason not to be happy. You may as well look at it the way it is; we are spinning in space on a planet in an infinite universe that is believed to be 10 billion light years in diameter. You being resistant to events does not change the world, it only changes you down to the core of your being. The only thing you gain from being bothered by life's events is suffering. You are going to die, you may as well have some fun and be happy while you are here. Observe without judgement, sit without thought, smile just because, experience without analysis, let things be the way they are. A quiet mind is a powerful mind.

Your happiness will be tested and you will pass this test with flying colors as long as you're happy to the core of your being. Why wouldn't you want to be happy all the time? Yes it is that simple. By making this unconditional decision to be happy regardless, you are immediately on the highest spiritual path available to humans. Just be committed to not breaking this promise to yourself. If you want to be happy you must be prepared to let go of the part of you that wants to create the stories and the resistance.

Remember one thing as you catapult from the well: it is not events in your life that are the problems; it is your resistance to the events that make them problems. What is a problem to you is not a problem to someone else because you both choose to look at the same situation with a different perspective. It is quite possible to have no problems for the rest of your life. All you have to do is not resist anything, let everything be exactly as it is. When you look at life this way, there are no problems.

> **"It is not events in your life that are the problems; it is your resistance to the events that make them problems"**

What would happen if you decided to just consciously observe the world? If you did, this would feel more susceptible and unsheltered. This is because you really don't know what will happen next and your mind is so used to helping you, jumping in and giving you the narrative you need to feel comfortable. It does this by processing your current experiences and in a way that makes them fit into your model or perceptions of the past and your vision of the future. This is all done to help you create some feeling of control. This is your way of making sure everything is ok. The day will come when you realize the mind constantly talks to itself as a protection measure against uncertainty. This is the opposite of what you want to do, you want to live life, not force it into your little mental model. The world is unfolding every day and has very little to do with what you are thinking. While you are trying to keep your world together with this self-talk, you're really just trying to hold yourself together.

If you experience stress regularly you have to ask yourself, "Why I am resisting these particular events?" There are events that happen all day long that get no resistance. You see houses everywhere, you see lamp posts on the road, you see people walk by, children playing, all of these events cause no resistance from you but when you see a full moon it creates resistance and opens the blockage that you have been carrying around. When you think back to when you were younger, you remember the time when you caught your girlfriend kissing another guy under a full moon. Every time you see full moon now, it brings back a flood of negative memories and bad feelings; the disturbance is present and real. You must remove these types of disturbances to be balanced.

The world and the universe have precise balance. We need to be as balanced and powerful as the universe is. Have you ever wondered how earth simply floats in space, never moving off its axis? Have you ever wondered how the billions of other planets in our solar system that are 20 times the size of earth never hit earth and wipe us out? What about the fact that most of the other planets and stars are moving at light speeds and Earth just floats in space revolving around the sun and moon giving us life. It does so effortlessly and in perfect balance with perfect precision. We have all heard of the virtues of being balanced. The entire universe is in perfect balance and you need to be as well.

It is this type of balance that other people look for in their mates and relationships. If you are out of balance, (eg drinking too much, overeating, too angry, undereating, a workaholic or any of the plethora of things we can be fanatical about) you won't reap as many rewards as possible. If you are out of balance the only other people that will spend time with you are other out-of-balance people. So get control of yourself and be balanced. Use your God-given self-control and your discipline to give you the best opportunity for success and enlightenment. Before you head outside of the well, your job is to work on yourself. If you are in mental turmoil inside the well, you will be the same outside of the well. It's inventory time.

This is an inside job and the amount of time required is in proportion to how far off centre you are. You want to return to centre as quickly as possible so that you have the best relationships, realize the best opportunities, and live a full rich life alive with happiness and peace of mind. If you want to live the life that your mind has been telling you about for the last many years, you will need to spend some time and invest in yourself. When people start to create their daily disciplines that match their thought desires they begin to act in harmony with themselves. When people act in harmony with themselves the natural harmony of the universe joins in and accelerates the fl w towards your desires.

It has been said that relationships are hard, perhaps the hardest thing you'll ever encounter. We have all heard this over and over in our lives. This is wrong, we have been lied to and have been lying to ourselves. Yes, bad relationships are hard but **great relationships are easy**. We have all had a bad relationship. Think about it for a second; yelling, posturing, positioning, eye rolling, and all the questioning, constant scrutiny: it really makes you scratch your head. Now think about a really good or great relationship you have or had with someone. The complete opposite, relaxed, happy, listening, interesting, intrigued; inspiring a future of growth. There is a massive disconnect between these two types of relationships. Being in a bad relationship is proven to be really bad for us. Get out of it if you are currently in one and be vigilant about all who enter.

Why people allow mistreatment in any relationship is a mystery. I don't know how or why people tolerate mistreatment, allowing it for years and years, sometimes tens of years, sometimes close to a life time. Allowing mistreatment of any kind in any relationship is not ok and cannot be accepted or tolerated for any length of time.

Think about it, would you let your neighbour pop his head over your conjoining yard fence and start to scrutinize what you are doing? "Hey buddy, I don't like the diagonal of your lawnmower cut lines." Questioning your decisions, taunting you, calling you names and generally behaving with negative intentions towards you? Would you let your best friend dictate what you do, when you do it and with whom you do it? Of course not!! Then why do we accept this in some of our most important relationships. Why is it ok for our spouse to "unload on us", scrutinize our decisions, yell at us, call us names even, ignore us, or just generally behave with negative intentions towards us?

If you are in the middle of one these relationship you should take a good look inside. You should very deeply reconsider and be concerned about this relationship. No one should have to accept any type of mistreatment, especially in a marriage. Always remember that other people's stories and behaviours are simply their conscious interpretation of events.

What is really happening is out of their awareness. This is how they see the world and the events in it and now you are hearing about it. These are their perceptions of life. If you are with someone who sees life considerably different than you it will be difficult to sustain this relationship as the differences are on too many levels.

If there is one thing that happens more often than not in people I have spoken to over many years, it is that they stay in bad relationships for way way too long before they leave. It was made clear that these relationships had no chance of lasting but yet they stayed in them for many additional years hoping it would get better. The mind has a way of conforming to less than appropriate behaviour from spouses or close relationships. The way that some spouses treat each other would never be tolerated from any other person other than the spouse. Why is it ok to accept this unacceptable treatment from a spouse or anyone for that matter?

When these relationships go to this critical stage, couples would often go to professional counselling to shore things up. After interviewing a few marriage counsellors it became clear that two patterns emerged. First, in a large majority of cases the relationship had suffered too much damage and could not be reversed. Second, in the other relationships that continue there were some minor brief changes that lasted a short period.

This is to say that it is difficult to change people at the core of their beings. People inherently believe that they are on the right path, that everything is ok within, and it's "not their fault." It is built into some people's DNA, that they can see no fault of their own. They see no fault or take any personal responsibility for the breakdown in a relationship or the condition of their lives. We see this all of the time in society. When one of the recently separated spouses is angry and letting everyone know how bad the ex-spouse was. How she was dogging him all the time, how he didn't pay the bills, she was lazy, he had a drinking problem, she never worked out, blah blah blah. It's always the other person's fault with no accountability.

Don't run from this responsibility, this is strength and is where true power comes from. True power comes from realizing life doesn't always go the way we want it. True strength comes from being completely all right when life knocks you around or you make mistakes. Why? Because you are steadfast, powerful and rooted in the middle ground. Here, there are no tempest storms, here you sit, enjoying the undisturbed serenity that is your life.

Become accountable for being a strong character when no one is looking. Become accountable for what you say and how you feel. Become accountable for what time you get up, what time you go bed, your daily habits, removing negativity and not letting yourself down. Become accountable for being authentic to yourself while not letting yourself down. Strength, confidence and swagger are rooted in personal accountability, regardless of what happens.

This is why self-mastery is so important because it is up to you. Once you start to reveal yourself to yourself you will soon see that your way was not the only way. Your way was all you knew which is why you went that way. You didn't know any other direction to go in. Once you see that there are many better ways you will be forced to take those paths because you have enlightened yourself. Once you begin a new path to your fulfillment, new more exciting paths will open and you will become robust in joy and opportunity. These are the natural laws of the universe. Working from the inside out is the only way.

People should not have to change who they are to fit into someone else's box. They should change the person not the box. If anyone tries to be in relationship where they are fitting into someone else's box, there is very little chance of this relationship surviving. People need to be themselves to manage relationships well. You cannot change someone else, you can only change yourself. Bad relationships are stuck lacking inspiration and in a lot of cases are just downright negative. There is no reason to believe that a relationship like this will survive nor should it. Changing the core of someone's being is not your burden to carry. You are too busy working on yourself. You can change people's daily habits, you can change their desires and you can change intentions but you cannot change who someone is. We are unable to alter anyone else's soul, it just can't be done.

"People should not have to change who they are to fit into someone else's box. They should change the person not the box"

There is no reason for anyone to have to change who they are anyways. Who they are is perfect down to their DNA level. They just aren't perfect for you. This goes back to what I was saying earlier. There is no need to please everyone or cater to everyone or connect with everyone. Connect with who and what works for you. If it doesn't work, don't connect and let go quickly and easily. Why would you want to sustain the pressures of a burdensome relationship?

It is in these burdensome spousal relationships where we will permit the most mistreatment, yelling, scrutinizing, negativism, posturing and a less than favourable atmosphere. These types of relationships are proven to be terrible for our well-being. We have to ask ourselves why one's partner in a marriage has such a great influence upon the other's mind. Because the relationship of marriage brings people under the influence of spiritual forces and under such weight they become dominating forces of the mind.

Being in a negative relationship is not how we are supposed to live. We all yearn to be content, happy, joyful, lifted, exuberant and excited. Any toxic relationship will eat away at your soul and not allow you to rise to your authentic self. This is why you need to be super vigilant about the people you allow into your life and with whom you start relationships. Search for people who are positive, optimistic, energized, happy, enthusiastic, smiling and are not complainers. Stay away from the complainers. They will suck you into the darkness of their imbalance, their stage of weariness. You will be listening about their sore back, their blown out knee from high school, their stomach problems, their lack of money, lack of opportunities and their overall lethargy. They will literally drain the life out of you.

> **"Stay away from the complainers. They will suck you into the darkness of their imbalance, their stage of weariness"**

This is the last thing you need as you rise from the well. What you need is someone who lifts your spirits, someone who makes you laugh, someone who isn't tied up in the past, someone who lacks emotional baggage, and someone who is happy already. Always remember that you cannot get something from someone unless you have it already yourself. You don't want get in a relationship with someone who you think will make you happy if you are unhappy. You already need to be happy to be with someone like this; they simply increase your happiness. An example could be that you are unhappy and want to find a partner that is happy so that you can be happy. There is a hope that they will rub off on you. This cannot be the case, while they can have an effect on you, they cannot change how you feel inside. They may rub off on you briefly but the rub will only be brief until you are discovered. You need to go into the relationship happy, make sense? Go sharpen the saw before you cut down the tree.

"Give me 6 hours to cut down a tree and I'll spend the first 5 sharpening the saw" Abraham Lincoln

Your search for relationships of any kind should only include persons who are balanced in all areas. There are many things to cause people to be unbalanced: inability to show genuine interest in other people, lacking a loving/kind heart, living out of the past, incessant complaining, too much alcohol or drugs, gossiping, caring too much about other people's opinions, overinvolved and in other people's business.

"You will get that which you are ready for, you will get roughly your equivalent"

Make sure you are balanced and seek only other balanced people. Remember there is no way for you to find a balanced person and maintain that relationship if you are not balanced yourself. You will get that which you are ready for, you will get roughly your equivalent. This is why it is mission critical to work on yourself and take the time to invest in yourself before your emergence from the well.

Let's examine desire. Desire is a huge driver for people.

Everyone desires things in this world, whether it's food, lodging, sex, money, health, purpose, etc. Desire is simply the will to repeat actions that once gave you pleasure. This is why we keep repeating the same things over and over. Drinking alcohol is an example. People enjoy drinking so they go to bars or restaurants over and over again. Exercising makes people feel good and is desirable so they do it over and over again. Working and making money allows us to live in a home and have heat and lights, this gives us pleasure, so we keep working. We want to relive the pleasure we derived from the activity as it was originally. It is because we are constantly in pursuit of pleasure that it makes sense to try and repeat events that originally gave us pleasure. Be careful because chasing pleasures can easily steer you off course.

People want certain pleasures and to live a certain lifestyle. We want to have nice clothes, nice housing, be fit and healthy, have a nice car, work at a nice job, go on some holidays, have a recreational property, and have some friends we can hang out with along with buying some cool things. Take a look at your list, that's a lot of pleasures you want and none of them come for free. As you decide on the pleasures to enjoy and actively pursue, remember that the more pleasures you want the longer it will take to achieve them. There is a certain disciplined and consistent work ethic that is required to have all of these desires. One can't sit around doing very little and expect to have the finer things in life. It will require some sacrifice plus some focused and disciplined effort to get these things. You have to be hungry though, you have to really want it.

The challenge with chasing desires is that is that when we don't gather the desires as quickly as we want, we start to create a little anxiety inside. The mind starts to turn the pressure up assigning a time line to the desires. The amped up mental deadline increases the pressure to the point where we start to question if we have what it takes to get there and doubt sets in.

Once even the slightest amount of doubt enters your mind about whether you have what it takes, its physical counterpart in the form of apathy will emerge and you will be defeated. The smallest amount of doubt will kill all efforts that you have put into chasing your goal. Doubt will kill almost everything in its tracks. A person who doubts himself would be like a person who enlists in the ranks of his enemies and bears arms against himself. He makes his failure by himself being the first one convinced of it.

Do not doubt yourself because the effect of doubt is the beginning of the end. Doubt can cause people to stop putting in the effort that is required to get them to where their mind believes it should be. They become unbalanced and unhappy slowly filling with tension. When we stop doing what is required long enough, the negative consequences begin to appear and we become disappointed internally. Sometimes in life, what we enjoy is not always good for us. People enter the valley, become depressed and even commit suicide only because they made the wrong decisions for so long that life spiraled downwards and they never recovered. The number one reason for failing personal change is people become so disappointed in themselves for consistently making the wrong decisions over time and fail to make the changes necessary.

You don't want to have to work too hard to get out of the well. This shouldn't be some huge monumental task. You are a couple of good decisions away from being on the offence again where that powerful stride is on display. And then your victories will motivate you to accomplish more.

To have the best opportunity of success though, always be on the alert for the unassuming **Double Work Load Effect.** This is the devil in disguise. What can happen very easily is you can double up the amount of your work required to get to your goal. You can stack more and more work on yourself if you aren't careful. By "missing a day" or "not feeling like it", you are deciding that you are prepared to do today's work and the work you missed yesterday. You have double the work to stay even. This is detrimental to the outcome of your focused goal. You could effectively in the end, double the work that is required. It is the same as spending money that you don't have and accumulate debt. Now you have to pay your bills and pay down your debt. It can be stiflin .

As you journey out of the well to finding your authentic self, keep this fact in mind: you manifest what you think, you manifest how you feel and you manifest your entire existence here on Earth. Always remember that you get to "make-up" and create who you are with no opposition from anyone. No other species on Earth can do this, only humans. You can literally change the person you were yesterday by simple acts of thought.

"You are a couple of good decisions away from being on the offence where that powerful stride is on display"

You may have pigeonholed yourself into thinking that you are a specific person but you're not. You are free fl wing energy that is always and forever changing. You are who you say you are and no one gets to tell you any different. No one gets to tell you who you are, only you. So make sure you make yourself into a great person, take all of the characteristics that you want and tell yourself that is who you are and start behaving that way. Start speaking that way, dressing that way, walking that way, loving that way, working hard that way, eating properly that way. It becomes who you are.

By pure thought, that is now who you are. Amazing isn't it? Once you employ these actions, you will actually become that person. You must stick with it; it will take time, but not as long as you think. Don't look back. The only thing that will throw you off course is if you stop the disciplined daily habits that are required to be this great person you have concocted in your mind. You have inside you already what it takes to be great and you know it. Don't let yourself down, do not lie to yourself as it has tremendous consequences.

You weren't born with anything different than people who do great things are. When we execute our daily habits, it opens the door to do something better tomorrow. Life will slowly shuffle you along until you have reached all of your desires. Having good daily habits will ensure that the growth process will proceed healthily and happily in a rapidly increasing ratio. This is much easier than the path of most people which is trying make things be what they are not. It is unnatural to not be that which you are.

"You have nothing to hide, make the choice to be truly free"

The fear of leaving the comfort zone is so great that people can become paralyzed. The comfort of the well is so safe and secure. You always know what's going on and there are few deviations. The fragility and fear allows you to remain safe and not have your resilience tested. It enables you to keep your vulnerabilities inside where you think they belong. You think that if you jump out of your comfort zone all of your vulnerabilities will be on display. That is because they will be on display for others to see and they should be on display. You have nothing to hide, make the choice to be truly free.

Without your insecurities removed, you will never get to your authentic self. There will always be a part of you that harbours weakness and doesn't permit true power and full authenticity into your life. Remember vulnerability is power.

Always remember that you are hiding something within yourself that is stopping you from personal growth that nobody cares about but you. No one cares about your insecurities but you. Not only are you hiding inside yourself, you are not giving yourself the opportunity to overcome them and move on to the next stage. The next stage cannot be reached if you are hiding stuff inside or lying to yourself. You want your vulnerabilities and your fears to be tested in the open.

This may seem counterintuitive but is completely required for you to take your life to the next level of greatness. What you end up finding out is that you become closer to people when you let them inside to have a peek at "those little fears". Allowing people inside brings people closer together. Why? Because we are all the same and your insecurities are the same as everyone else's insecurities, only some people have jumped from the well and managed to remove their fear of what other people think. Shutting off the rest of the world and living in the well is not the answer. Preparing yourself for the jump out of the well is the answer. The emergence will come with all sorts of tests, but tests that you actually want. These tests will acclimate you to the outside environment. It is these tests that you want and accept and look for. The tests will come in two forms: internal and external.

The tests from within will arrange themselves around the mental structure you have built for your life. Your structure is built out of your analytical discrete thoughts that are in relationship to each other. You do this to feel some degree of control of the world. We see this mostly in our efforts to make the unknown known. Everyone draws up their perfect scenario of how the day should look, what should be involved in the day, the pace of the day and how the day ends up. You have it all figured out, even the future. We all create our own reality and how we think it should be. This mental model has become your reality.

The inherent problem with this is that now you must struggle day to day to make sure everything fits into this model you have built. If it doesn't fit, what are we going to do? When events don't quite fit into your model, you create resistance. If anything happens to challenge how you view life you argue, defend yourself, posture or rationalize. You are unable to fit what is happening into the model you have built. The problem is that your mental model doesn't incorporate reality. You need to go beyond the limits of the model you built.

"When events don't quite fit into your model, you create resistance"

If you want to go beyond your limits, ask some hard questions. The first one you will want to ask is, "what influences along the way helped me form this model of myself? Why did I build this model?" Have you ever built a model that is moving along great and producing exactly what you wanted until it gets rocked and really tested when something goes wrong? The amount of suffering that results can be frightening. It is remarkable how this powerful model you built was really just a house of cards that spared you from nothing.

After your decrepit model gets hit, the struggle to get back some type of your model's semblance can be difficul . What you begin to do is pull the mental model around you like a shawl so you can get back to your comfort zone. If your model is broken, it is time to change the model. Keep reading, the Middle Ground bears much fruit for its weary travellers.

The other resistance you will encounter is from yourself. You will continue to tell yourself whatever stories you have made up to justify staying in the well. You want to get out of the well, you just don't know how to because you have told yourself lies for most of your life to avoid your full emergence. It is quite a mistake to suppose that we must restrict ourselves to develop greater power or usefulness. All that is required is within you and waiting to emerge, just a little push and reap the rewards. There will be no better joy in finding yourself through all the incessant chatter.

You are prepared exactly as you are, right down to your DNA level. If you are telling yourself any different, you are lying because you are afraid to do the work necessary to find your authentic self. You are using this as an excuse. Yes it takes time and is not easy, not everyone gets there. You will never find yourself if you don't jump from the well and get out of the comfort zone. Take the first step, do it, jump, call that person, start a financial plan, start a health plan, join some groups, spend time where happy people are, go to the gym - just get out of the well and let yourself shine with absolutely no fear of hopping back in! Especially now that you know what to expect and how to deal with it. There are no more excuses available other than you simply don't want it badly enough. If that is the case, no worries, just do us all a favour and stop complaining if you are going to do nothing about it. Those who are working hard at it don't want to hear the whining and complaining about what you don't have. That is a one way ticket to depression.

Why do people actively choose to remain in the well?

Mainly because they have concocted a story about themselves in their mind that will say something like the following: "I am just too shy," "I am not fit enough", "I am a loner", "I'm not good with people", "I'm not pretty enough", "I'm not outgoing enough", "I don't have enough money". There are a hundred things people tell themselves to avoid anything slightly resembling discomfort. People tell themselves these stories of falsehood so they have a built in excuse to do nothing about their current situation. My suggestion is get to work on removing these fabricated stories or excuses and let your authentic self-emerge. Do not be afraid of being powerful, do not be afraid of how much work it takes, and do not be afraid of being responsible for the state of your life. We have all been gifted with these incredible qualities, use them wisely and to your benefit

As you assemble your plan to take the leap, you must take your environment very seriously. The environment that people live in is mission critical to wellbeing, health and happiness. A study was done using rats. Rats were put in a cage with two bottles, one filled with heroin and the other cocaine. Soon enough the rats became drug addicts and there was a high volume of overdoses; no big surprise there. In analyzing the results, the question arose, what would happen if we gave them the two exact bottles of heroin and cocaine but also gave them a great environment to live in. Give them lots of cheese, a few wheels to run around on, lots of food and water and friends so they can have lots of sex. As the study continued, drug addiction was down 50% along with drug use and overdoses were minimized greatly. The results clearly indicated that being in stable environment is extremely important. It is the environment that we eventually end up becoming. You create your environment but amazingly your environment creates you.

You must ask yourself a question: Who do you want in your inner circle? Who are the people that you admire and want to spend time with? Make sure that only these people are included in your circle. It is your choice who you spend time with. It is not arbitrary, you get to choose. Make sure you choose the right people. How do you determine who the right people are? You use the Three Strike Rule. Using this rule will be a sure-fire way to tell if you want to spend more time with anyone. Remember that it is not your job to connect with everyone, it is a numbers game. The more people you see the more people you won't connect with but when the connection occurs it will hit you over the head like a sack of hammers. It is well worth the wait for great solid connections. The reason you will know the feeling of a great connection is because you know intimately the feelings of a lousy one.

It's not always easy jumping from a well but, get to the top and have a peek over, this is where your best self will live and thrive. The best part of getting out of the well is that you will get used to it, and it will become the new normal. Sure you'll take a few shots, a few relationships won't work out in your favour and you'll be wandering in your own head. That's perfectly OK, it's supposed to be that way.

Imagine having a quiet mind, one that only thinks and speaks of love, strength, goodness and human connection. A mind that sees sameness of all and beauty in everything. Imagine the doors that will open and the opportunities that will unfold in your life once you carry a balanced mind and a tempered soul. Once your mind has faith, swagger, belief, confidenc , it will take you to amazing places with sheer delight. Whether you believe it or not, we are all connected and are all the same. Gather the skills required for human relationships as it is these that will make the world truly a wonderful place to live in.

Now that the mind is quiet and you have removed the disturbances, you can fully emerge from the well. You are now the centre of distribution, distributing your joy, happiness, kind words, uplifting messages, big smiles, love, laughter, confidence and an overall message of well-being and compassion for others. The reason you remained in the well is because you were hurt, in pain, suffering or afraid.

We have never been off the right path, we just have been walking backwards instead of forwards. As we begin to walk the path in the right direction, we shall find that it is nothing other than the path to happiness, joy, peace and power. Once we begin to live naturally within ourselves, attaining our desires and pleasures becomes easy. The reason we experience anxiety, restlessness and weariness is because we are trying to be or do something which is unnatural to us. We are trying to be someone we are not. When we begin to live naturally, we shall find everything we desire and more. Our daily lives will become complete joy and we shall spread enlightenment to those around us, becoming a beacon of shining light. Your radiance will light other people up, you will be seen as you are, an absolute miracle that is pure love.

This state of being will attract all of the other people who are like this. You see, these types of people hang out together because they can't be bothered to hang out with people of lesser wisdom. In order to hang out with great people, you must be in balance. As you come out of the well, make sure you are working on your balance. You can't expect to hang out with balanced peopled if you remain unbalanced. Work on your mind first, get your mind and state of being right. If you have baggage from the past, you must get rid of it before you can bring the greatness into your circle.

The reason for this is because you won't be able to maintain the great people in your life, they will see through you and your weakness will be exposed. The people at the top also had baggage, believe me, you are not alone in your struggles, everyone takes a beating in life but the people at the top have chosen to leave their baggage behind so they can release their authentic self; now it's your turn. Do whatever it takes to come to terms with your past and the feelings you still have for the situation. The only way to remove this baggage of yours is to FORGIVE. Either in person, on the phone or in your mind. You must forgive yourself, the other person or other people.

If you don't work for it you don't deserve it and you won't get it. It only comes to those who work hard for it and pay the price that is required for its attainment. You have to shape your character and callous your mind in order to grow. You'll get rejected by a few people, who cares? There are eight billion people on the planet, move on to the next one. As you stretch your spirit, you will wrestle with yourself in your own mind; so what, we all do. Just remember, sit back, listen to your thoughts objectively, and let them pass through you; pay no attention to most of them. Let the thoughts move through you and out the other side with no action or further contemplation, they will disappear.

"Act on the thoughts that stir your mind with joy"

We have 3,000-4,000 thoughts an hour. Some of them, in fact most of them, will be no good bordering on useless. Act on the thoughts that excite you and give you fuel that you need. You know the ones, the thoughts that give rise to your soul and energy to your body. You can literally feel these thoughts as you have them, they excite you. These types of thoughts are the thoughts that you must give further consideration to and act upon. Act on the thoughts that stir your mind with joy. Act on thoughts that offer challenge, inspiration, happiness and personal development.

As you act, it won't always work out your way but at least you are coming out of the well-armed knowing this, knowing that life doesn't always work out the way you want it to. You are going into these actions knowing how to handle people better. Being amongst the frogs is soon to be a joy, one that you will soon not be able to do without. You'll be lily pad jumping with them, swimming in groups, eating dinners out and enjoying yourself like there is no tomorrow. This is what frogs do and this is what humans do; we are designed this way. Take the time to learn how to enjoy it, it will most certainly elevate your life.

Accept love as your strongest asset, one that you should practice often and place a lot of emphasis on. Why? Because if used properly, it will not only change you, it will change others and can change your world. The most powerful people in history, the people society writes and make movies about, put tremendous emphasis on selflessnes , inclusiveness and love. Mahatma Gandhi, Dr. Martin Luther King Jr., Mother Teresa to name a few. Why are they revered and talked about so much? Because they made it to the highest peak and they got there with selflessnes , inclusiveness, compassion and love. They didn't just show up on the top of the mountain, they used compassion, kindness, empathy and strength as their climbing tools.

These are the tools of the hero, the powerful, the infl - ential, and the game changers. They started with nothing different than what you and I came equipped with, a head a body and a mind. They too showed up on the earth, just like you and everyone else with no manual or game plan. But these people, like many others, soon realized the best game plan for their life was one that centred on servitude, humanity, love, kindness, giving and togetherness. Let's make this the benchmark of our lives. Let these attributes be your guide to the decisions you make, the goals you set, the plans you draft and how you spend your life. They will not lead you astray, I promise. On the contrary, they will create the foundation of someone worth writing about. It is a certainty by the testimonial of those who have gone before us.

You don't need to change the world, but rather use these sound characteristics as the foundation of your authentic self. Use them to change your environment, your soul and your perspective on life. Allow the love to fl w freely without regard. Once these characteristics are embedded in your soul, there will be nothing anyone can say and no situation that would have you surrender your position of love and power.

Love has been scientifically proven to be the most significant emotion we have, larger than all the others combined. That being the case let's make sure we embrace people, see the best in everyone, wish people well, be kind to strangers, speak only positive words, add value to your life, the life of others, your community and the world at large, for you are out of the well, armed with the knowledge required to handle life outside the well. Go for it, it is yours for the taking.

Once you take the first few steps forward, the magic will open up. First it will be slightly uncomfortable, then it will be kind of enjoyable, then it will hurt again and, after enough time, it will be an absolute joy and you will become extremely fulfilled. There is an inner and an outer side to everything. The quality of the superficial mind, which causes it to fail in the attainment of the truth, is the willingness to rest contently with the outside world. So long as a person fi es his or her attention only in the superficial, it is impossible for that person to make any progress in knowledge, which is the root of all life.

"Once you take the first few steps forward, the magic will open up"

We are all exactly where we are supposed to be in this life, don't think differently. It is you and only you that can create a different future; this is your job now, create the future of your dreams. It is your time to take yourself from where you are to where you need to go. It doesn't matter where you are starting from. From the lowest depths of existence to the greatest heights of success, a person's life is always an exact reflection of that practical stage which has been reached in the perception of the divine nature and of that person's own relation to it.

As we reach full perception and our authentic selves, our inner being expands and the old bonds and limitations which had no existence in reality in the first place, fall off us as we enter into peak happiness, power and strength of which we had previously no conception. The only way to fully realize your potential and get in touch with your authentic self is to move forward and into the uncomfortable zone, wherever that is and at whatever level that is for you. Just jump, you won't regret it. In fact, it will be the best move of your life.

Upon emergence from the well

You can fully expect joy, happiness, peace of mind, love and fulfilmen on the full emergence from the well. It is bestowed upon all who take the leap of faith. An understanding about life and understanding about yourself will emerge. Remember that the root of all things is life. Not as we recognize it in particular forms or manifestations, but as something more interior and concentrated than that. It is a free soul, a soul that sees no problems, a soul that knows peace and happiness, a soul that is at rest and satiated. **There is a name for this state**

of being, it is called enlightenment.

To allow the universe to fl w around you without analyzing or evaluating every situation and person in it creates a freedom that is reserved for those who take the time to work at it.
This state of being isn't granted to everyone and some people
never realize it. Some people go through their entire lives being
restless, scattered and discontent. You see them all the time,
the ones that lay on the car horn unnecessarily when you're
merging lanes in your car, the ones that impose their will on
you unnecessarily, the people that can't generate a smile to save
their lives, the people who complain about nothing, the ones
who become snappy over the littlest of things; unenlightened
people are everywhere.

I have never met anyone who doesn't yearn to be happy,
peaceful, vibrant, joyous and powerful. They just don't know
how to do it and haven't spent the necessary time to figure
it out. This state of being is available to anyone but there is
a requirement and that requirement is some work and some
time; you must be patient. If you are willing and committed
to putting in the work, you too can achieve a state of being
where there are no problems, a state where you are perpetually
in fullness in the moment along with enjoying a state where
happiness underlies it all. You don't need money, a fast car, a
beautiful girlfriend or wife, a big house or a high paying job.
This state of being is available to the rich as it is the poor; in
fact, it's free. The less you have the easier it is to engage this
state of being. When we become bogged down with too many
material items, it creates a weight that can suppress our growth.

The spirit has an inherent generic character with which
we must comply if we would employ it for our own good, and
this can be summed up in one word, "goodness". When you
see the world through the lens of love and goodness, the world

listens to the nature of your song. Energy attracts like energy. When you're in a state of enlightenment and fulfillment, the negatively disturbed people keep their distance, the angry and negative stay away from you because that is opposite to your energy. This law of the generation of power by attraction works on the spiritual level as well as the physical dimension and acts with the same mathematical precision on both. This power is generated by how well your soul and your thoughts are connected. Each person is the centre of their own universe and has the power by directing their own thoughts to control all things therein.

We encounter different energy fields when we are around other people's proximity. The energy field theory says that there is an invisible vibratory field surrounding all living objects, including human beings. The field is created by how we process our experiences and by how we think about wherever we are in the world. At certain levels of consciousness, the energy vibrates slowly, at other levels of consciousness the energy fiel vibrates fast. There is a continuum along which varying levels of consciousness are responsible for creating the field of energy. Think about it for a minute. You can talk to two different people and have two completely different vibratory states. Let's say the one person is over involved, stressed, anxious and consumed by themselves. The other person is in the moment, happy and curiously engaged in the conversation. There will be a noticeable difference in both vibratory and excited states of being. Keep this in mind because we all have the ability to feel another person without touching them.

Happiness is when your thoughts and your words and your actions are all the same - Gandhi

Apply this law of spirit to our own individual worlds and see it not as an external source but an internal source that can be manipulated and maneuvered into creating the life we desire. Use this amazing ability to your advantage. Become a master of yourself, work on yourself constantly, whether it's reading, meditating, exercising, sleeping, laughing, building, hugging, loving, giving, helping, hanging with friends; whatever it is, do it always and often.

The emergence will be the greatest event of your life. Without getting out of the well, you will never know what's on the other side. The magic is in the unknown; lean into your greatness, take a seat at the wheel of your beauty. The beauty is in what you do not know yet, it is not hidden in what you know. Allow your inner being and soul to create a new life as a butterfly does once escaped from its cocoon. It will be a lot easier than you think, take one step at a time.

The past and the future will slowly dissipate and dissolve. I'm not saying don't plan for the future; planning and goal setting is very important. It is the constant thought about what you don't have that will dissolve. You will be able to truly enjoy the process and not the finish lin .

Always remember that our beliefs determine our behaviour, and our behaviour determines our character and our character determines our results. Another way to look at this is "Be-Do-Have." Most people put these in the opposite order, like "Have-Do-Be." People think that if they could just *have* more, then they would *do* the right things, and then they would *be* who they want to be. Abundance works opposite to this. If we want to *have* more, then we should start by *being* better people; in order to do better we start *doing* better things, which leads to having more of what we want. When we become who we were born to be, living authentically, every resource imaginable becomes available to fulfill our oals and desires.

The more you let go of yourself and just commit to the task that you have set, the more your spiritual energy will increase within you. Once you align yourself with life's outer fl w, the more the beautiful inward fl w of energy will naturally strengthen. Letting go of one's self-centered thoughts and emotions is all that is needed for profound personal, professional and spiritual growth.

TAKEAWAYS

- True success is not measured by obtaining the result. True success begins the minute you have committed to the process of achieving the goal.

- True success is who you become along the way as you strive for your chosen goals. The success lies in how the process of achieving the goals makes you. Who you become while you chase the goal is the important thing.

- Why? Because the joy of the end result is short-lived and the process of getting there often takes years. Shouldn't it be the opposite? We should toil away at our goal for a couple of weeks and the feeling of success should last for years. Sorry, it is the other way around, I didn't make up the rules.

- Success doesn't care what you look like. It is a level playing field

- Sometimes you need to be at unrest with where you are in life. This is the seed of progress.

- There is absolute perfection in you. It is really important you get that. You do not need to be modified or changed in any way. If you want to make some changes in your body or mind, be prepared to work diligently at it for a year or two. Be prepared to work for that which you want.

- The price of happiness is self-control and discipline. Both free and abundant.

- Look at your failures in the opposite. See them as set-ups and not setbacks because that is exactly what they are.

CHAPTER 7

RELATIONSHIPS ARE A BIG DEAL – THREE STRIKES

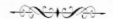

How other people treat us and how we treat other people has a significant impact on the quality of our existence here on Earth. It has an impact on how we feel, what we think, decisions we make, how we perceive life, how we internalize life and how we react to everything in between. In this chapter we shall deploy the three strike rule that, if followed, will not only free you from scrutiny, questioning and negativism in your life, it will allow you to be around the right people who only want the best for you. Those who want to help you, see you grow and be creative.

Whether you are looking to let a new person into your life or you have been married thirty years, applying this rule can save you a lot of time, freeing up your energy for the right people to come in and above all hopefully give you some perspective on your relationships. This is ground zero where you can create a clean slate and have a fresh canvas to paint the story of your life, your way.

We are all the same in that we need the love and admiration of people around us. Very few people like to live in isolation; at the very least acceptance is essential. Most of us like to have at least one person or many people around us most of the time. We see this bonding in our relationships, marriages, businesses, sports teams, the community and globally. Being with other humans is just part of the deal. Consequently, we need to be careful with who is allowed to influence us and with whom we spend our time. We need to vet the people we choose to surround ourselves with, otherwise, anyone can get in and infiltrate our precious energy.

Our levels of happiness are in direct correlation to the people in our lives and the relationships we have. This being the case, we need to have a vetting or radar system that protects us from the wrong people and only permits people who make you better and APPRECIATE YOU. This system must have parameters that govern the decisions on who is allowed into your life and who has to be removed. Letting the wrong people into our lives can cost us great deals of time and energy that we can never get back. Most, if not all of us, have been in a bad relationship and are familiar with not only the wasted time but the mental suffering that was endured.

> *"Our levels of happiness are in direct correlation to the people in our lives and the relationships we have"*

Before we get into the vetting system you need to know how important relationships are in our lives. **Relationships are mission critical to your overall wellbeing and happiness.** We have been studying and tracking the impact that human relationships have on us but none like the Harvard Study of Adult Development that has gone on over the past 75 years with over 724 men. This is the longest standing study that we know of. It is so long that they are now studying the 2200 children of these men. The study was conducted using two groups. The first group were boys from the 1930's Boston's poorest neighbourhoods. They were chosen because they were from some of the most disadvantaged circumstances. The second group were sophomores of Harvard University. Some of these men are now in their 90's and sixty of the original seven hundred and twenty four men are still alive and still participating in the study. The study followed these men, interviewed them on the phone and at their homes, drew their blood, had copies of their doctor's reports, spoke to their families and their children. It is an exhaustive quest to measure happiness, wellbeing and overall health. They studied these men from their teens to their old age. Here are the indings:

The number one thing that made people happy and healthy was not about wealth or fame or working harder. The clearest message that resulted from this 75 year study is this. **Good relationships keep us happier and healthier. Period.**

Here are three big lessons about relationships from the study as quoted by Dr. Ron Hebert.

Social connections are very good for us and loneliness kills. It turns out that people who are more socially connected to family, friends and community are happier, physically healthier and live longer than people who are less well connected. And the experience of loneliness turns out to be toxic.

People that are more isolated from people than they want to be find that they are less happy, their health declines earlier in midlife, their brain function declines sooner and they live shorter lives than people who are not lonely. You don't necessarily have to be alone to be lonely. You can feel lonely in a crowd or lonely in a marriage.

It is not just the number of friends you have and it's not whether you are in a committed relationship but it is the quality of your close relationships that matters. **It turns out that living in the midst of conflict is REALLY bad for our health.**

High conflict marriages without much affection turn out to be very bad for our health. Perhaps worse than getting divorced. Living in the warmth of good relationships is protective.

The study went on to try to predict who would grow into a happy healthy octogenarian, defined as someone form 80-90 years old. After they had gathered all they knew about them at age 50, it wasn't the cholesterol levels that successfully predicted how they were going to grow old, it was how satisfied they were in their relationships. The people who were the most satisfied in their relationships at age 50 were the healthiest at age 80.

Good close relationships seemed to buffer these people from the slings and arrows of getting old. The most happily partnered men and women reported in their 80's that on the days when they had more physical pain their mood stayed just as happy. Adversely, the people who were in unhappy relationships on the days when they had more physical pain reported that the pain was magnified y more emotional pain.

The third big lesson learned about relationships and our health is that good relationships don't just protect our bodies they protect our brains. It turns out that being in a securely attached relationship to another person in your 80's is protective.

In relationships where they can really count on the other person in times of need, those people's memories stay sharper longer. The people who are not in relationships where they felt they can count on the other in times of need are the people whose memory declined.

Good relationships are good for our health and wellbeing. This is not new wisdom. The question is, why is it so hard to get and so easy to ignore? The answer is because we are human, what we really want is a quick fix, something we can get to make our lives good and keep them that way. Relationships are hard and complicated. It's messy with the hard work of tending to family. It's not sexy or glamorous. It's also lifelong. It never ends. The people in the 75 year study who were the happiest in retirement were the people who replaced work-mates with playmates. Meaning the interaction and relation-ships with others remained constant in their retirement.

Many of these men who started out with the study from the beginning wanted to be wealthy and famous; this is what they thought would bring them the good life. Over and over, the 75 year study clearly indicated that the people who faired the best were the people who invested into relationships with family, friends and community. So what about you? Let's say you're 25, 40 or 60. What might leaning into relationships look like?

The possibilities are almost endless. It might be something as simple as trading screen time for people time or livening up a stale relationship by doing something new together such as go for a hike, long walk or date nights, or reaching out to that family member to whom you haven't spoken in years because those all too commonly family feuds take a terrible toll on the people that hold the grudges.

The challenge we face when entering a new relationship is that people don't tell other people around them about the "real them" the myriad of bad decisions they make, the questionable behaviours, the long string of broken relationships, the lack of ambition, or the addiction whatever it is. Humans are really good at having problems and we are even better at concealing them from others.

The problem when entering a new relationship is we don't get the benefit of an interview with their families and friends, we don't get to hook them up to a lie detector test and we cer-tainly can't get a look into the character shaping relationships they grew up in. So essentially we know nothing about them other than what they tell us about themselves. In some cases, we don't have the benefit of enough time so we can at least see the other person behave for a while. You need a full year to get to know someone well and two full years to get all the bugs revealed.

We do know that people always paint a rosy picture about themselves so it is without a doubt when you enter into a new relationship you are not receiving the full picture of the other person. Quite the opposite, we hide our little secrets, insecurities and vulnerabilities and only tell those around us about the positive areas of our lives, how well things are going. Humans are designed to protect themselves, both physically and mentally.

This goes way back to the caveman days where self-protection was paramount otherwise you would die. Self-protection hasn't gone anywhere now that there are no dinosaurs or physical threats. Instead we protect ourselves by presenting a false picture into the world and those in it. There is a name for this and it is "inauthenticity," defined as anything that pretends to be something it is not. This is part of our mainstream lives not only between ourselves in person but also all over social media. Everyone wants to be seen as having a wonderful life and showing everyone that their life is working out great; "no worries here."

We all know that their life is just like ours and, as beautiful as it is, is far from perfect. You don't hear people talking about or posting about their business failure, divorce, bankruptcy, their children failing at school and doing drugs, or the fact that they are 45 lbs. overweight, stressed out and haven't had sex in months, the constant yelling and name calling, or husbands attacking wives or vice versa. You never hear these conversations or see these online posts which is most certainly a good thing but much closer to the truth.

Knowing that you are not going to get the "full story" from others, you must rely on their behaviours to show who they are. People always reveal themselves by their behaviours. There can be discrepancies between what people say and what they do. This is the pocket where insecurities lie. When people say one thing and do another they are insecure about whatever that gap is. That gap is their weakness, their blockage, their disturbance.

"You must rely on their behaviours to show you who they are"

That gap will soon become your problem in the new relationship, a problem you didn't ask for and a problem you don't want. While we want to give people the benefit of the doubt and let them prove themselves, keep a close eye on this gap. This is where any problems will come from. The three strike rule, which we will discuss in a moment, will let you understand the difference between the two and act accordingly.

Let's examine human posturing and how to understand the nuances involved. Posturing can come in many shapes and sizes. Our thermometer around whether someone is posturing us is to feel it. Your natural human instincts will notice any person who has negative energy towards you; listen to your instincts. The human mind can read facial expressions in as little as seventeen milliseconds; the first sign of posturing is facial expressions. When people posture, their eyes change and become more intense. Their eyebrows can furrow, their head tips to the side or perhaps they look upwards. This is the first sign someone is coming your way.

"The human mind can read facial expressions in as little as seventeen milliseconds"

Fairly quickly thereafter, the physical body language will appear followed by distinct choices of negative wording and phrasing. When you put all three of these together, you have someone who is attempting to posture you. Posturing people is not ok and cannot be tolerated under any circumstances. Whether you are letting someone new into your life or you have been married 30 years, posture and positioning on people is **not OK**. It is disrespectful, lacking empathy, aggressive, manipulative and quite frankly can border on bullying.

Other signs of posture are language changes, tone of voice increases, body positon adjustments, overall energy changes, all creating guilty feelings as well as manipulating information and people. This is the time to feel your instincts, this is the time to simply observe the posture, notice it occurring and rest briefly realizing that everyone does it including you. As you observe the posture, try to understand why they are posturing. It is almost always because they want something or have attached emotion to that which they are opposing. Someone posturing you is them revealing their insecurities to you.

You're not going to be a punching bag for their insecurities and you must see this as their insecurity and look to help them. After all, you have just met and you need to see how deep this insecurity runs. If someone you are with has chosen to posture you as their method of communication, you need to keep a very serious eye on this. The good thing is: it's only strike one.

"Someone posturing you is them revealing their insecurities to you"

No one is allowed to put you down, posture you, call you names, question or scrutinize your moves. Nor are they allowed to look at you with the "crazy eyes", or physically get in your space if you don't want them there. You must not allow this. We all disagree sometimes and have differing opinions. This is perfectly fine and healthy. What is not ok in any relationship is for someone to mount an attack because they have a different opinion or belief. Great relationships are based on the long standing premise of "no posturing".

Sometimes when entering a new relationship you can learn over time that the other person has a propensity to enter life's extremes. That is to say that you "find out" your partner occasionally dwells in negative behaviours. The signs can be obvious as they are early. Depending on the severity of the imbalance or behaviour you have a couple of choices. Before the choices, let's all agree that there are cases where there is only one strike; where someone has acted completely offside and it's over. Do not hesitate to remove anyone from your life who creates an act of massive extreme.

The events we are talking about here are the scenarios that aren't horrible but certainly not good and something you will not live with for long. The scenarios where someone's desires get a little carried away. The extremes that you won't accept in your partner long term but will give them a second chance. The appropriate choice in these cases is to spend some time with the other person to help them with the extreme behaviour, this assumes they don't like their imbalance either. Be compassionate and work together to strengthen the relationship. These are the moments where you can form very strong ties with someone. Growing and nurturing a great relationship is a magical process. During this process just keep an eye on the three strikes rule, let it be your compass.

Don't be the person who is dogging the other person, don't be micromanaging people. This is exactly what will happen if you hop into a relationship where you don't like someone else's behavioural patterns and you try to fix them past the three strikes rule. Your job is to find the right relationship in the first place even if it takes many tries. Don't settle for second best in any relationship.

"Don't be the person who is dogging the other person, don't be micromanaging people"

The litmus test or benchmark of any great relationship is how much time is spent being negative, moving laterally and being stagnant. This is where the 90/10 rule comes in. Use this as your benchmark for all of your relationships. Ninety percent of a solid relationship is fl wing, creative and full of energy. It operates on the highest level of love and respect, it is built on creativity, building and helping at large. All of your relationships should be founded on the rule of 90/10. We all deserve to be in great relationships. Great relationships rely heavily on respect, happiness and positive forward thinking.

The 10% of the 90/10 rule is negotiation, compromise and dealing with the fact that we are different people with different pasts, we have been raised by different parents and have different views on life and how we see and deal with it. The 10% we are ok with the other person being who they are and understanding that they will have different views, perceptions and opinions. This is perfectly natural and only serves to enlighten each partner further with other perspectives.

We have all heard that, "there are billions people on earth and there is no one quite like us, that we are completely unique". This is fact. In which case, we must acknowledge that none of those eight billion people think exactly as we do all the time. In general, we all think the same about life in that we want food, water, love, health, some money and some security. Other than that, we all think differently but our way of thinking is not always right. The way we think is based on how we were raised, what happened in our past and how much time you have spent working on yourself, making yourself a better, more valuable person.

I have always said, if you want to know why people behave in a certain way, a sure fire way to understand is to go meet their parents. We become who we are largely based on who our families were, it's just the way it is. We take the good with the not so good when it comes to how we are shaped mentally in our youth. It's a full package. People behave the only way they know how, it is programmed into them. Let's give them a break. None of us landed here with an operation manual or guidance system. We are all just doing the best we can with what we have been given or gained along the way.

"You can only reach your authentic self if you are in the right relationships"

When we acknowledge that we are far from knowing everything or in control of everything, and we are not right in our thinking all of the time, it frees the mind to be open and accepting. It gives the mind the freedom to allow the right information in. Once this level of freedom is reached, it allows us to go into our relationships knowing that 10% of the time we are going to need to give, negotiate (not posture or position– stay in control of yourself), compromise and really listen to what the partner or the relationship is saying to you. This is where you get to strengthen good relationships and make them great. This is the same pressure that shapes a diamond. This 10% is a prerequisite to forming great relationships and absolutely necessary. You can only reach your authentic self if you are in the right relationships. Really make sure that you are in relationships that lift you up, inspire and challenge you to be your best. The foundation of a great relationship is mutual respect for each other.

The three strike rule is a way of governing how a relationship is going and the prospect of it lasting. It is a way to make people accountable with great ease. Using three strikes is easy to understand for both parties and creates little friction when removing yourself from a relationship. Once the three strike rule is understood by those involved the disconnection only makes sense regardless of what happened. It is sometimes in our best long term interest to not enter some relationships. It is also in our best interest to remove yourself from relationships that aren't even close to the 90/10 rule. Bad relationships can vacuum out the strongest person's energy. We waste so much time in bad relationships, time that we'll never get back. What personal or business relationships you choose to enter into must be vetted very carefully using the three strike rule.

We are human beings so no one is perfect and everyone makes mistakes but no one is allowed to position or posture themselves on you. When it happens once, this is *strike one*. Let's use the example of someone questioning your character or behaviours. This is the most common form of posturing. When you see and feel someone posturing or circling you with negative thoughts and emotions, recognize that they are only behaving based around what they know, how they were raised and what baggage they have from their own life experiences. Always remember that as humans, we simply project our own insecurities into the world and direct it to the people around us whether we are right or wrong.

"Bad relationships can vacuum out the strongest person's energy"

Let me give you an example. You were cheated on, lied to and deceived by an ex-girlfriend or boyfriend. You are hurt, vulnerable and in a weakened state. You take your insecurities into the next relationship. You then proceed to question and barrage your new partner with your insecurities and baggage. This is a very common situation when entering a new relationship. We tend to carry our insecurities around with us from relationship to relationship.

The other person will project their insecurities onto you at the first snif of misbehaviour. You sit there confused, having no idea what the other person is referring to. If you haven't done anything wrong, you must see this for what it is. It is simply another person casting their insecurities into the world and more particularly at you. This is what people do all of the time, this is common amongst humans. This is where you need to take charge and let them know that you are not a sounding board for all their insecurities in life. You weren't put on Earth to accept behavior from other people that is less than well intended. You must let those people know that you will not tolerate this behaviour and tell them about the three strike rule - yes flat out tell them this is what is happenin .

It might sound funny telling someone about the three strike rule but it is important to let people know your expectations and your boundaries. If you fail to let people know your expectations on how to treat you, how do you expect them to treat you? You will be treated by them through their filter of the world and in a lot of cases through the lens of their disturbance. They will treat you how their parents treated them. They will treat you how they treat everyone else and sometimes how people treat other people is unacceptable.

You must not allow your future to be determined by this person's wayward messages and behavioural patterns. Don't be ok with someone posturing you and treating you poorly. Stand up for yourself and be strong otherwise you have effectively told that person that it is 'A OK' to treat you however they feel. It is a slippery slope that does nothing for anyone but create a negative environment and further permits the action.

"Those who control their environmental influences and thought patterns are the masters of their destiny"

No human owes another any degree of duty which robs them of their privilege of building thought habits in a positive environment. On the other hand, every human being is duty-bound to remove themselves from an environment that even remotely tends to develop negative thought habits. Only the strong survive. We are unable to be strong when surrounded in negativity. Those who control their environmental infl - ences and thought patterns are the masters of their destiny.

The reason there are three strikes is because it allows you to determine if this is a pattern or an isolated incident or anomaly. People are allowed to be wrong and make mistakes and treat people how they feel. Remember, as long as you are not doing anything terrible, heinous or criminal, there is no right or wrong. There is only your perception of the situation and how you choose to see it based on your limited belief set that may have been planted in you from a young age. A lot of our beliefs, perceptions and values are programmed into us from an early age and can be a self-fulling prophecy.

A great calm will come over you when you release yourself from the burden of always having to be right. When you realize no one is right and no one is wrong, it will allow you to take better stock of your relationships. It will allow you to see how often you and your partner are divided and have differing views. Differing opinions and viewpoints are reasonable and expected in any relationship. It is how the relationship deals with, handles and negotiates these differences that matters. How any relationship deals with turmoil and difficulty will be the ultimate test of relationship survival.

Let's take a look at another person that was raised in a less than perfect environment. They were born absorbed into a world where anger and yelling was common place, it was the family's modus operandi. It was how this family spoke to each other and behaved. They will quite naturally learn that yelling is used as language and behaviour and in turn they will arm themselves with this emotion, it will be their "go to" emotion and they will apply it to any human that comes along. **This is the reason there are three strikes.** We are humans and sometimes don't always put the right foot forward with the right intentions, it's just the way it is, no free passes here.

We have all behaved in a way that we would like to take back or have a "do over". We are all guilty of saying things we shouldn't have said and behaving in ways that we shouldn't have. We're just humans and perfection is not our thing; measure *people by their intentions if there is doubt*. The beautiful thing about life and the people in it is we always tell other people who we are by our words, actions and our behaviours making it very easy to vet who is about to enter our lives or who is currently in our life. Behavioural patterns emerge in all of us. That is to say, we can get to know people pretty well and easily, within a year or two or even sooner. These behavioural patterns must serve as the barometer of the relationship you are currently in or are about to enter.

"Measure people by their intentions if there is doubt"

Strike one is basically a free pass. If you are in a new relationship or changing an existing one, the first time the "crazy eyes" or "verbal arrow" is shot into your chest, this is the time for your Mohican stand. This is the moment you get to establish yourself and stand up for your personal sovereignty. These are the moments you get to exercise your character. It is you that will be showing the other person what behaviours you allow in your relationship not the other way around. This strong stand is where you get the final say in what treatment comes your way. This is your moment to be the steward of your life.

The flip side of this stand is that it shows the other person you care about them and they are meaningful to you and you are prepared to forgive them in the hopes they are able to change that particular behaviour. Remember you weren't put here on Earth to connect with everyone. In fact, you will really only truly connect with a few. Do yourself a huge favour and connect with people who don't posture you, get up in your grill, attack you, always questions your moves, motives and decisions or are just generally negative and complaining.

When we do learn about other people by their behaviours, it becomes an opportunity to decide who we let into our lives. This is how we shape and design our life with the intention of happiness. **We get to decide who is in and who is out.** I'll bet you have let people in that you wish you hadn't. If you are not able to keep the three strikes rule in mind, the wrong people will enter into your life and your boat will take on water moving you further away from where you want to be.

Speech and decision-making is another virtue that humans have been gifted with. We are the only species on planet earth that has cognitive reasoning abilities. Dogs don't, birds don't, no animals do, just us humans. Use this to your advantage. Listen to people, watch people very closely as they will tell you who they are and show you how they behave. If you let a person talk long enough they almost always end up talking about themselves. If you possess a few people skills, try asking some questions about other people, try to find out a little bit about them, take a little dive. Believe me, they are more than happy to talk and tell you all about themselves. This is your time to find out about people. Be inquisitive, be curious, and learn about others.

In fact, the essence of the book, "How To Win Friends And In luence People", by Dale Carnegie, one of the top ten best-selling books of all-time, is just that: if you want people to like you, get them talking about themselves.

Strike two: If a particular behaviour happens once, it is likely to happen again. As an example, if you were to yell loudly at someone in a heated discussion, the chances that you will repeat this behaviour are very good. If you've never lost control and yelled aggressively at someone, the chances of you starting now are remote. Behaviour is literally defined as a series of repeated events. What I am saying is that, if someone behaves in a particular way, there is a high possibility that they will act this way again. This is where you need to be careful. Why do you need to be careful? Because the person is showing you how they behave, they are showing you first hand who they are. You need to pay careful attention to this. This is your litmus test.

At this point you have given the person strike one telling them you don't accept that behaviour or the way they treated you. Now the same behaviour occurs again. This is where you must deliver "Strike 2" and let the other party know that, again, this behaviour is unacceptable to you. You need to let them know that it is perfectly ok for them to act that way if that's what they want, but their behaviour is just not for you. You must explain at this point that you are uncomfortable being treated that way or that you are uncomfortable with their behaviour and you will not tolerate it.

"Be very careful who you allow in your life and who you interact with daily"

If **strike three** happens, that is to say the person repeats the same behaviour a third time after you have been very clear, careful and gentle with them, you must leave this relationship. If you don't leave, you will be injecting into your life a poison that will cripple your wellbeing and overall happiness. If you don't leave, not only will it take a long time for the relationship to dissolve, robbing you of further energy, it will take a while to rebound back up to your greatness again. It is a double edged sword. Be very careful who you allow in your life and who you interact with daily. People's greatness can be vacuumed from them if they are around negative people all the time, spouses included.

At strike three, the other person is very clearly disrespecting you, your wishes and your requirements. They are telling you this first hand by their behaviour. No one needs to tell you they are disrespecting you when their behaviour already does. This is a sure sign there is no connection and will not be a connection. Do not fight this, never fight what you know. If you find yourself saying to yourself "he doesn't mean it", "she won't do it again" or "it will get better" or "if I just do this than they will stop", you are lying to yourself to protect your perception of what you believe the outcome should be. It won't get better or change, why would it? Don't be an enabler. This is who they are. Again, it is ok for them to be that way, they are simply not for you, move on.

Do not tie your good luck and worth to the outcome of any relationship; let it fl w, let it be, let it ferment, percolate and watch it grow or not. The outcome will be the outcome. If it is a great connection, guess what, you got yourself a great person at your side. If the relationship doesn't work and you end up issuing the third strike, guess what? This relationship isn't for you. Move on!! Without this terribly important connection, the relationship will dissolve and never make it. Do not tie yourself to the outcome of a relationship, just let it be what it is. Give 100% to the relationship, be your authentic self but do not compromise who you are for someone who isn't on board with who you are. If someone is unable to respect you on this level move on in a hurry.

"Do not tie your emotions and worth to the outcome of any relationship"

To this point, you have been very careful with them to let them know, in no uncertain terms, that you will not be staying in the relationship if they continue their wayward behaviour. The response to your caring attitude is they keep doing it? This tells you that they don't care much about you and the relationship if they are unable to take your guidance on how you want to be treated. Why would you want to be with someone who is disrespecting you? You are worth more than that!

The reason there are three strikes is because after someone does something three times, they have revealed a pattern. A pattern is defined as a regular and intelligible form or sequence discernible in certain actions or situations. You have seen the other person's actions that established a pattern of disrespect for you. To think this behaviour will change is delusional and you pinning your hopes to it changing is only inviting suffering.

There is a funny mechanism of optimism in all of us that tells us that "this will get better", "they will change", and "they told me they won't do it anymore, so they won't". We often see this in the form of someone behaving badly. Let's say someone is yelling at their spouse for whatever reason. The person yelling feels bad about their behaviour and cries a bit and apologizes and tells the other person that they won't do it again. I would be very cautious here, the guideline is that if it happened once, it will likely happen again.

"The best predictor of future behaviour is in past behaviour"

Let me tell you, if you never lashed out in anger, well, you have never lashed out in anger. It just hasn't happened and will more than likely never happen. If you have hit a woman you have shown the propensity to hit a woman and there is a very reasonable chance that you will hit a woman again. If you are angry and a yeller, you won't just become a quiet relaxed person who doesn't yell. Remember, everyone is perfectly free to act how they choose. They are just not free to act that way around you because you won't accept it.

The best predictor of future behaviour is in past behaviour. Don't put too much emphasis on the words, focus on the actions and behaviours, they will tell you the truth. Time and behaviour always reveal the truth. Actions and behaviours are your guidance system to all people you meet. If you don't like the way someone behaves either towards you or in general, recognize that the behaviour will not change and this is just how they choose to behave. No one is allowed to disrespect you or put you down or call you names or posture you. FULL STOP.

RESET

Human compassion is a great characteristic to have in any person. Compassion can be how strong relationships are born and forged. If you genuinely care for people, then we shall reset the strikes back to zero and start fresh after an acceptable amount of time has gone by. The reason is that when you get hurt in life, as we all do, there are different levels of pain. There is a big difference between a girlfriend breaking up with you and your dad leaving the family when you were a child or perhaps the death of a loved one. One carries a deeper longer lasting pain. This is a pain that is difficult to understand if you have always had your father around or you've never had someone close to you die. This is where compassion for other people comes in. It doesn't give the fatherless person an excuse to treat others badly but the situation does call for some compassion and understanding.

In the case of resetting the strikes to zero, let's say your partner has showed remorse for their behaviour and has stopped behaving that way for 6 months. Remember changing our hard wired behaviours along with parental and societal pre-programming can be very difficult to do. If you love this person, you will reset the strikes and give them another chance, assuming the behaviour isn't too radical. You are not perfect either and have your fl ws. Giving someone a second chance can have its benefits to you down the road as well as showing someone you love them.

For those who are in long term relationships that are flat, not inspiring and filled with negativity and posturing, my advice is simple. Leave it. I don't know why anyone would want to be in a soulless negative relationship; it makes no sense. Leaving a long term relationship that is soulless is the only option if you care about your happiness, well-being and the condition of your soul. You cannot have both an inspired relationship and a soulless negative one, it's just not possible. One has to go and it may as well be the bad one.

Everything will be ok as you think about leaving a bad marriage or relationship despite all the things you may be making up in your mind. Don't talk yourself out of leaving. You will have money, you will have a roof over your head, you'll find another person, you'll get a job, and it too shall pass. If you choose to leave a negative relationship and go on a mission to better yourself and not wallow in the mud, don't make it any harder on yourself by fabricating potential future scenarios that haven't happened.

"There have been many catastrophes in my life, most of which have never happened." - Mark Twain

Many people will simply talk themselves out of leaving a toxic relationship by fabricating questions about the future they don't have answers to. This is a sure fire way to remain stuck in this relationship. Not having the answers to where the security will come from, where will the love come from and what does the scary post relationship future look like, is ok. You are not expected to know the future, just don't be afraid if it.

What has been proven over and over is, after one leaves a toxic relationship, the amount of joy and happiness is way more than the person could have imagined. Sure it will be difficult at first with a lot of unknowns but once the dust settles in 6 months to a year, the joy can be overwhelming now that you have your spirit back and a clear head.

The long-standing question is, why do we get into the wrong relationships with the wrong people and stay in them for a great deal longer than we should? Almost anyone who has been through a separation or divorce or relationship split of any kind will tell you that they should have left the relationship years before they actually did. If your current relationship isn't even close to the 90/10 rule you need to take some serious inventory.

There is an inherent built-in human desire for people to be with people so that we can fulfill our needs of love, security and happiness. As a result, we start looking for physical companionship at an early age and it never stops until it is satisfied, at least in perception. When we are young, we don't know ourselves very well, we don't know who we are. There is a lack of worldly experience that doesn't permit us to have enough time to grow into ourselves and have wisdom. True growth and understanding of yourself is realized through experience or time on Earth. Knowing yourself and having wisdom go hand in hand. To know yourself, you must have wisdom and to have wisdom you must know yourself.

When you don't know yourself, you can't know others. This is the how we start relationships that fail. We don't know ourselves. We haven't demonstrably established our core principles, values, morals and behavioural patterns leaving us prey to whatever people throw our way. Without knowing exactly who we are, it becomes very easy to be pushed around, manipulated and postured upon by others. Knowing yourself is knowing these values inside and out so that when they are tested, a red light goes off and says this is not the person or relationship for you because they clearly don't know who you are. What we end up doing is chasing around people and relationships we don't necessarily even want or know under what condition we want them, all in order to fill the holes in our unce tain minds.

"When you don't know yourself, you can't know others"

It is these perceived voids that leave us stressed at night and wondering what to do and how to do it. Let's say we are single and feeling a bit lonely, what do we do? We go out and look for someone who can provide us with a reprieve from the loneliness along with some security, love and camaraderie. When we find a person or relationship that has a fighting chance, we play it out to see if it is a fit; we give it chance. What ends up happening is we choose a person that hopefully will make us less lonely. By doing this, you have only insulated yourself from the lonely feeling. Once the external situation, in this case the new relationship, fails to protect you from what's inside, the problem will be back. You have asked the wrong question to yourself. You have asked yourself, "What can I say or do to make me feel not so lonely?" You are not asking, "How do I get rid of the problem?" you are asking, "How do I protect myself from feeling it?"

This is why you are an inside job and must be worked on from the inside out, not the other way around. Until these core disturbances or insecurities are removed, happiness and fulfil - ment will be elusive. You will end up carrying the same baggage from relationship to relationship. You can't keep looking outward for answers that only you have within; it is a waste of time. This is what people do, they let their internal insecurities affect their behaviours and in turn run their lives. It is what we have inside that we think on. It is what we have inside that we speak on. It is what we have inside that we act on. What we have inside is who we are.

If you have been cheated on or betrayed, you will be very sensitive to a new relationship when they work late, or are out for drinks with friends, or away for the weekend. The insecurity of your past disturbances will wash over you like an ocean storm. The questions of "who were you with?", "where did you go?", "what time were you home?" will soon follow. The disturbance or insecurity you carry inside is now running your life. Do not doubt your ability to remove the root cause of the disturbance inside of you. Make the choice to not have your life run by the weakest part of you. Make the choice to truly love because you truly love and recognize the power it wields. Don't love because you are trying to avoid your inner problems.

"Make the choice to not have your life run by the weakest part of you"

With age should come hindsight and wisdom? Wisdom only comes through the lapse of time and cannot be imparted from one person to another, except through the lapse of time. Wisdom is not guaranteed, it only comes to those who form positive thought patterns as a dominating force in their life. People who are dominated by negative thoughts or are negative never acquire wisdom except for that of an elementary nature.

What is wisdom? Wisdom is the ability to harness nature's laws so they serve you. It is the ability to relate yourself to other people to gain their harmonious, willing cooperation in making you get that which you desire in life. Adversity, failure and age are the only way we can gather and use these instincts.

These are nature's universal laws through which it imparts wisdom to those who are ready to receive it. Once wisdom is established, you must act in accordance with it. This is the inexorable working of the **law of harmony.**

Without wisdom and harmony, relationships can be challenging as there is no compass or benchmark for behaviour. We end up defaulting to our sub-servient behaviours that have been engrained in us since childhood, and these often aren't good enough. Relationships are challenging and require a great deal of maturity and hindsight to keep together and alive. If you don't have these attributes, relationships can take a change for the worse, very quickly, at the first sign of stress. One of the biggest stressors in relationships is the questioning of the other's character. There is a tendency for partners to not believe or trust the other's character or words in times of trouble.

If you don't know your own character, values or morals and a friend or partner questions you, you will feel insulted, take it personally, get angry, probably lash out and try to flip things around on that person. Take the time to analyze your behavioural patterns, look inside at your virtues, your grounding principles, your non-negotiables, your morals and integrity. This will fortify who you are, this will make you powerful. Remember, you are the lion in wait, you are the one with the key to your happiness and authentic self. When your core soul is strong and someone questions your character or postures you, you will pay no heed to them and send that person packing if they keep it up.

Personal development is an inside job; all of the answers are within and around. Inward focus will provide the love, the security and the safety that is required to self-develop and move forward despite circumstances. All of these beautiful qualities already reside in you, they just need to be unlocked and set free. You are love, you are secure, you are strong and you are the lion in wait. Work on yourself first, get back to basics, eat well, speak easy, sleep, rise early, meditate to clear and slow down your mind, exercise, work hard, create, imagine and inspire yourself to new heights of greatness. Remember, you must know yourself before you can know other people.

TAKEAWAYS

- We teach other people how to treat us. We don't allow other people to treat us how they see fit

- **Good relationships keep us happier and healthier. Period.**

- **It turns out that living in the midst of conflict is REALLY bad for our health.** High conflict marriages without much affection are very bad for our health.

- When entering a new relationship people do not reveal themselves. People become revealed over time through their behaviours and their actions. One year to get to know someone, two years to work it all out.

- We must preserve our energy at all costs. Never allow someone to posture you. Posturing is not ok and not an acceptable form of communication. When you feel it, stop it in its tracks.

- We must only accept solid relationships. It is not your job to connect with everyone. If you don't connect with someone leave them, it's OK.

- Follow the 90/10 Rule. Great relationships are easy 90% of the time. The other 10% is where differences lie and we must compromise, negotiate, discuss and really listen to understand. Great re

- lationships allow no room for posturing and are built on mutual respect.

- Using the Three Strikes Rule makes it easy to examine and assess anyone or any relationship that you are about to enter. It establishes your boundaries and protocol

- Your relationship will provide guidance and some type of measuring stick on how far off balance it may be.

- Don't allow other people to cast their insecurities onto you in the long term. Their problems are their problems, they need to deal with them, you don't.

- Don't chase things around. Get straight in your own mind and let things chase you. There is a huge difference here. Being unbalanced will only get you more imbalance.

- Wisdom is not guaranteed, it only comes to those who form positive thought patterns as a dominating force in their life.

- Once wisdom is established, you must act in accordance with it. This is the inexorable working of the Law of Harmony.

CHAPTER 8
DISCOMFORT – THE PRICE OF FREEDOM

It's important to realize that quite often, when you get a little bit uncomfortable in life and stretch yourself to really "go after it", that is when you truly begin to reside in the lofty space where the world's most successful and enlightened spend their time.

Successful people have made a living and a life out of enjoying the results of a journey that has, more often than not, involved plenty of risk. Without fear there is no courage, they act courageously yet with caution, act aggressively but with compassion, and make their moves from a position of strength while also showing a fragile vulnerable side.

These enlightened people operate on inspiration, and, though they face the same potential pitfalls as the rest of us, they get after it and enjoy the process. They do not operate with excuses at the ready nor any serious thoughts that they can't do it. Don't be one of those people who never experience this type of bliss, the wave of adrenaline that comes with pushing all your chips into the middle of the table, simply because you are too afraid to explore the unknown.

Imagine, for a moment, that you could map out your life – from Point A, when you're a small child, to Point B, as a senior citizen as if you were simply programming the GPS system in your car. The computer would instinctively know exactly where you were in that moment at Point A, in grade school, or playing in a sandbox, or sleeping in a crib next to your parents' bed and, once you punch in your final destination, out shoots a slew of directions and instructions, mapping out your next 80 years or so.

Every detail of your life, however small, would be there laid out before you. You'd know where to go, what girl to talk to, what classes to take in high school, what investments to make, which city to retire to, and so on. It would, no doubt, be a very comfortable existence and a potentially lucrative one, if that GPS system happened to tell you in which tech stocks to invest in, or on what team to lay a large Super Bowl wager.

> **"Enlightened people operate on inspiration, and, though they face the same potential pitfalls as the rest of us, they get after it and enjoy the process"**

You'd know exactly how your professional life would shake out, thus ensuring every career move you make, and every business you start would be the correct choice. But where's the fun in that? You'd be successful, sure, but wouldn't you find ourself bored if you knew everything?

The phrase "it's the journey, not the destination" may be something of a tired cliché, but it's a well-worn phrase for a reason because it's true. And the fact of the matter is this: we don't have a crystal ball or a GPS system for life because we aren't supposed to have such things. That's not how this road trip we call life works. We are not supposed to know how we are going to get to where we're going, and we're certainly not supposed to know the route. We'd miss a lot of excellent side-trips and shortcuts if it were true.

Also, if we knew how something was going to turn out in advance, there is a very real chance that we'd pass up on doing it. If you knew that you'd start a business that would ultimately fail, but you'd learn valuable lessons and make important connections along the way, would you still do it? Or, if you knew your marriage would end in divorce, but you'd still get a couple amazing kids out of the union, would you still pop the question? Conversely, what would you choose if you knew that a new venture would lead to success and wealth, but would be such a difficult journey to get there that you would have to compromise your personal health and relationships to achieve it? Would you have second thoughts about it?

These are all tough-to-answer hypotheticals, and hypothetical is exactly how these quandaries should stay. We can't know the answer to these many questions before we start, so instead, we're left to our own belief in ourselves, and to faith or, to quote the title of a more-than-200-year-old Italian opera: *La Forza del Destino*, which, roughly translated, means The Power of Fate. To put it in a more practical metaphor, it's also a concept similar to driving across the country in the dark. You can turn your headlights on, and power 'em up as high as you'd like, but you still aren't going to be able to see all the way from Los Angeles to New York. Instead, you'll only be able to see about 50 feet in front of you. In reality, it's all you need.

As for the rest of the country? Well, you'll get there when you get there. In the meantime, you just have to trust that the next 50 feet will unfold just like the last 50, or better.

Faith is the belief in the unknown and an act of trusting that the process will get you what you need. When you accept that faith and fate exist, and you start living in that reality, the comfort of knowing that the next 50 feet will be just fine is the beginning of true growth. You will begin to see life differently, and you will see opportunities differently, and see your problems, big or small, with a different slant. The challenges that you once thought were obstacles will now become catapults forward and a new source of power and strength.

"Faith is the belief in the unknown and the act of trusting that the process will get you what you need"

Take chances, move outside your comfort zone. Explore. This is where the real magic truly lies. The direct result of doing things that make you uncomfortable is you build a belief and resilience in yourself that tells yourself you CAN DO IT. It creates the momentum that powers you on to the next challenge until you are at the top. It is simply one win after the other, stacking up the wins that unlocks the forces inside you.

It goes against most people's inherent way of thinking, but it's important to take these chances and, in many cases, do the exact opposite of not just what others are doing, but what a section of your brain is telling you as well. The ability to push through that risk-averse part of your brain is why only a few are truly successful.

Successful people aren't afraid to move beyond their comfort zone, but for the average person, making a move such as this can be incredibly diffic lt. It has always been this way and is, in large part, a survival instinct. It's in our DNA.

There are two people inside our minds. The first is the practical person, who, in modern times, is seen as the responsible one. The person who gets a good job, pays the bills on time, and makes conservative moves. The second is quite the opposite. That self is the one that wants to take risks, be adventurous and risk it all (or at least some of it) for even more.

The "no pain, no gain" self, if you will.

There's one problem with this philosophy of course and you may have discovered it already: taking these risks is difficult. If stepping out of your comfort zone was easy, everyone would do it. Start with small steps for the first few months until the resilience is built up inside you, getting you ready for the next challenge.

When I competed in my first triathlon, I remember going to the local pool to work on my swimming. I am not a big swimmer, I love the water but have never done much more than float around in it. I remember the first day showing up at the pool and doing one lap. I was completely knackered, breathing heavy with my mind racing thinking, how in the world am I going to do 60 laps when I can barely do one? I knew there was only one way to handle this and that was to do two laps the next day and three the next day and so on and so forth until I was able to do 60 laps. So that is exactly what I did. I kept showing up for months increasing my lap total per day every day until I did the required 60 that was involved in the triathlon.

Writing my first book was a daunting task I can assure you. I simply followed the same process as the triathlon; little bits every day for as long as it took to win. Two years later I published my first book and two and half years after that my second. My point is that whatever you decide to choose as your goal, the process to attain is the same for all of us. You just have to make a plan, roll up your sleeves, and build your daily habits around that plan. The old adage is true, "how do you eat an elephant? one bite at a time."

There is no other way to handle this and many of the endeavours that you will encounter in your life. You must start with small daily steps for whatever amount of time is required until you win. If you are lonely and introverted, don't start by hitting up the local night club; this will only serve to frighten you from going back. Start with something less intimidating, perhaps the local toastmasters group or maybe join a local running club or something where like-minded people gather. You need to work up to your goals.

It's a difficul step, no question about it, but consider that nearly every successful person has forced him or herself to take that step, and it becomes slightly easier to rationalize. When you're ready to take this step, it will no doubt lead to the Promise Land, full of happiness and a renewed faith that you had no idea was inside of you this entire time. Once you gain the confidence that comes with succeeding you'll smile more, be happier, laugh louder and have a life of abundance. However, if you never take that step over the edge, you'll never know what was truly, potentially in store for you. The only way to find out is to summon the strength and courage to step forward.

No matter what unknown you are stepping into, whether it's thinking of moving your business in a new direction, asking out that girl, leaving that long term soulless relationship, or quitting your dead-end job and chasing your passions. You already know that deep down this will be the best thing for you. But you'll also be scared, and let me tell you, you are supposed to feel scared. You're supposed to be uncertain and second-guess yourself. What you *shouldn't* do, however, is fill your head with negative thoughts and only imagine the negative outcomes, talking yourself out of it. These are your true moments of inspiration that you need to tackle head on so let the positive feelings wash the negative thoughts to the side. Don't talk yourself out of these decisions, no matter what your mind tells you. Remember, the mind is a master at distraction and deception.

"I believe that each of us has the power to overcome this penchant for safety"

I believe that each of us has the power to overcome this penchant for safety, and if we push past it we all have the ability to change our lives, whether that means financiall , personally, or otherwise. Here is what you need to do the next time an inspirational thought hits you. You know the ones, the thoughts that make you smile, or give you goose bumps. Ignore, as best you can, the adrenaline that shoots through your body. This 'adrenaline dump' is always the first thing to occur in these types of scenarios. Use it!! It's God's boost of energy saying. "Go for it!" Give yourself a few minutes to allow the adrenaline to fl w through you and then explain to yourself how much better you'll feel if you were to take act on this feel good thought and make this latest inspiration a part of your life.

Don't back down from it, and under no circumstance should you tell yourself anything negative about the opportunity for one full day. Try not to let any negative thoughts even enter your mind such as "I can't", "it will be too hard", "it will take too long" etc. Then, after that 24-hour period is over, if you still find yourself wondering how much better your life would be if you took the risk-in-question, it's clearly a leap worth making.

From there, take the next step towards. Make a plan around your inspirational thought and from there, the next step, and then next. Stay focused on the 50 feet in front of you, and the next 50 and before you know it, you'll be clear across the country.

"There is no finish line and (that) life is a dance to be danced"

I've achieved much of what I've set out to do, and it's never been because I had any predictive powers it's because I've made a conscious effort to live in the present. I've made conscious decisions to build plans around the pleasures and desires that I have. I've just enjoyed the journey and the surprises that have come along, with faith in knowing that there is no finish line and that life is a dance to be danced. And even if the end result isn't exactly how I pictured it might be, I'll have learned an awful lot about myself and grown as a person along the way.

Place your focus on the process of getting to that goal and always remember, it's not reaching the goal that ultimately counts, it is about what and who you develop inside yourself that matters. While you're shooting for this goal, you are building new skills, learning to be disciplined, and forming the habits of a champion. Once those habits are cemented within you, they're transferable to any future dream or endeavour and will serve you well in the long term. Passion begets passion. If you're not living passionately in all areas of your life, how can you logically expect to have a bright, passionate, exciting, successful future? These things you want, whatever they are, will not happen "just because." You have to work for them, and if you don't, if instead you find yourself in something of an abyss of mediocrity, then it's time to make a change.

The answer is simple, get back to the basics. If you find yourself off centre in whatever area(s) of your life, get back to basics. Change your routines, wake up earlier, be healthier, stick to a plan or a schedule, be involved, read books, listen to podcasts, get enough sleep, Eventually, you'll see measurable results.

"Failure along the way is simply tempo-

*rary, and in the long run, it won't make the
slightest difference"*

By leaping into the unknown, there are going to be a few
bumps and bruises along the way, ones you can't even conceive
of in the beginning, but that's OK. Don't worry about it, believe me, nobody else will either. We tend to care far too much
in today's world about how we look to other people, and we
don't want others to see us fail. Perhaps it's an ego thing, or an
embarrassment thing, who knows. Maybe it's a combination of
both. If we do trip ourselves up, it's also worth it to just take
the loss; own it. Yes, maybe you failed, but you failed trying
to do something awesome, and it didn't decrease your enthusiasm, so all is well. It's better to go a hundred miles an hour
in the wrong direction than it is to go 10 miles an hour in the
right one.

Failure along the way is simply temporary, and in the long
run, it won't make the slightest difference. What will make the
difference is that you kept going anyways. When you're standing at the top of a huge staircase, nobody remembers that you
tripped over your shoelace on the third stair. Of course, now
that I've said all this about taking risks and pushing yourself
beyond what part of your brain tells you is possible, it's important to note one more thing: it's key that you balance this
idea of your two selves.

If we leave the "other self" to its own devices, we're
bound to take our life savings to the roulette table and bet it all
on black. These are not the types of risks we're talking about;
calculated, "smart" risks are entirely different. As long as you
remain in good standing with your two entities and keep them
balanced, you should be able to obtain every goal you have,
and achieve every goal you set for yourself. What more could
you hope for?

TAKEAWAYS

- Act courageously yet with caution. It is better to be a lion that to be a sheep.

- Don't be afraid to explore the unknown. There can be much joy when you arrive somewhere you have never been. We are not supposed to know where we are going.

- Take chances, move out of your comfort zone.

- We are made up of two people, the practical one who is responsible while the other wants to take risks and chances and get out of the comfort zone. Manage these two minds as they both are wise assets.

- When thoughts that inspire you arrive, act on them. These are the thoughts that you need to pay attention to. You know the ones, the ones that make you start to dream, and the ones that make you think that "if I could only do that". Those are the magical moments that you must grab on to and run with.

- As you chase down your desires, you will develop the habits of a champion. Jumping from comfort develops new skill sets. Every time you jump, you learn. Every time you learn, you become more

- valuable. The only thing that concerns you is how you will look to others. Don't worry about that because NO ONE CARES. Just jump, you'll love it.

- Developing this type of resilience will be the backbone that will be needed for the next challenge. When you stack one win on top of the other, you achieve the things that you desire.

- If you're in a bit of a slump, change things up; change your routines, your daily thinking, your rituals and you will see measurable results in no time.

- Remain in good standing with both sides of your brain. Don't blow the life savings on the roulette table but don't be afraid, weak or trepidatious either. Don't sit on the sidelines and watch your life pass you by. This is what regret looks like and this is no fun.

Chapter 9
Achievement – Putting It All Together

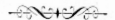

U p until now this has been a journey of the soul and understanding how to harness the massive energy it contains. We looked at how perceiving events and people in the negative can lead to molecular manipulation, leading to unhappiness and disappointment. We now understand how valleys and low points in our lives are created. We know how to avoid the valleys and ruts and stay clear of them. Up until now, we have looked at the importance of discomfort, why it is necessary and the rewards it carries.

We have learned how to treat people and how to teach people to treat us. We have also learned about how significant relationships are in our lives along with the importance of being happy. We have learned to allow life to be the way it is without interference, to live in the middle ground. We have gathered all of the necessary tools to take ourselves to the next level, where we belong. In the end it is achievement that makes us most happy.

Master achievers are those people who have an unwavering commitment to their goal and will stop at nothing to get there. Anyone can be a master in achievement. All it takes is some passion, some discipline, some human will and patience.

If you have these ingredients, you too can become a craftsman of your desires, a steward of you.

People achieve in all facets of life and professions, behaviors and life in general. You can be a master at teaching, singing, running long distances, juggling or being a great person who is full of life and exuberance. People master achieve at the Rubix cube, riding bulls, building companies, playing baseball, being educators, writing books, mastering electricity and even deep sea diving without oxygen. Do not confuse master achievement with making lots of money. This seems to be the way most people lean when they hear achievement; it almost always gets confused with money. Once you remove this definition from your mind, you soon see that you too can master achieve at anything that you have an interest in. However, if increasing your income happens as a byproduct of you becoming a master achiever, then all the better, but it should not be the primary reason for wanting to become a master achiever.

Achievement is not a mystery. Success is not a mystery. There are no secrets to success there are only systems to success. All human achievement is grounded in passion, curiosity, excitement, determination and consistency. Why not make this you, it will get you what you want? If that sounds like a great idea, one in which you're interested, then simply be prepared for years of work. You have the time; time is not an excuse.

"There are no secrets to success there are only systems to success"

You are going to be spending your time doing something while here on Earth, you may as well spend it like champions do. You are only asking 2-3 years of yourself in the beginning, in the grand scheme of things that is not very long. If you feel like you aren't important enough to have a great body, improve your financial security, have so much love its ridiculous, get a great job, and find the right person, be fulfilled, happy and joyful, well you're wrong. You know you deserve it and it's available to you. Give yourself 2-3 years of consistent disciplined behavior and it WILL happen. How can it not?

Here is the key: your time, thoughts and choices, must mirror your beliefs and the "why" behind it all; regardless of anything else. If there is a disconnect between your beliefs and your actions, you will get nowhere. Masters always believe in themselves and that they will succeed. It is this deeply ingrained self-belief that is the fuel for their fir . This belief is what keeps them going and won't allow them to stop. If they stop, they will have let themselves down and that is never OK with someone striving for mastery in this world.

> *"Don't let your wandering mind take you off course. Make the plan and work the plan until you win"*

Who is better than you at being you? No one. First, instill in your mind that you deserve to be the best and that you are the best. Ingrain the thoughts of you being the absolute miracle that has gifted the earth with your presence. Why? Because it is the truth and if you are telling yourself anything different you're wrong and lying to yourself; this will get you nowhere. You are perfect down to your DNA and you know it. All you are experiencing is your mind telling you that you want a little more stuff that you don't have already and that it's not quite content with what you have. The constant chatter about what you don't have, it's telling you that you want more money, more love, a little more sleep, a better job, a better car, a little more social life, a healthier diet, better clothes: it is just your mind that is restless and things need to be different. If you can just take your mind out of fift gear and down into third, taking the time to gather the right perspective, your focus will immediately shift to the process. If you are enjoying the process then you automatically win. Don't dwell on your desires. Don't let your wandering mind take you off course. Make the plan and work the plan until you win. This will keep your mind quiet and allow you to focus on executing the daily disciplines without fail.

You currently have everything you need right now and from here, all it will take is discipline, consistency and patience. There really is nothing to lose. Remember that nothing appears to change day to day but over a year or two, everything changes. Achieving anything in life all boils down to this one concept. **Knowing what you want and building your daily habits around that.** Whether it's writing a book, having the body of your dreams, having the mind of your dreams, starting a business, doing a marathon, it only takes good daily habits that are executed with discipline, consistently over time. It is that simple. The only thing that gets in the way of this is YOU.

For the reason of your choosing, you may have already told and justified to yourself why you can't or won't do it. You either have a well sharpened concocted story about yourself at the wait or there is some pain, disturbance or blockage that hasn't been released. Whatever the case, it makes no difference, IT must go. Master achievers don't carry disturbances around with them and the only story they tell themselves is that they will win. They know how hard it is to summit the mountain so they remove all extra weight. You can fall off a mountain if you're not well prepared.

Master achievers build happiness in various forms for

themselves and others. They give back to humanity, they get up early, they help people, they grind, they relax, they stay up late if necessary, and they don't give up. Their commitment to themselves, to others and to the goal is clear and obvious. They do everything in their power not to let themselves down; they are real with themselves, and they don't lie to themselves. They are the people who, despite the criticism and negativity thrown at them, achieve anyway. They are the people who never stop, no matter how difficult a challenge. These achievers are disciplined in specific habits vailable to everyone.

What makes one person a master achiever and another person accomplish average things is whether or not these habits are applied with consistency; that is it. **Can you possibly imagine that consistency is the main difference between average people and high achievers?** We are all born with the same stuff, no one has more than the other. It is all just a question of do you have the longevity, the passion, the determination and consistency to win. We all have these characteristics but only a few exercise them patiently over years until their goal is achieved.

Master achievers realize that there is no time limit to their success. They understand that the universe has a say in the outcome and that they control only what's in their purview. People who achieve understand that despite having only so much control of the outcome, there are some things that they can control. They can control their work ethic, emotions, response to situations, mental toughness and resilience. When you combine these traits with a dogged determination, patience and years and years of serious toil, you have a champion. These characteristics are the backbone of all great achievers.

Greatness comes in thousands of forms. You can be a great community leader, friend, son or daughter, volunteer, organizer, investor, spouse, house builder; the list goes on. Greatness is not reserved for those that make the headlines or become rich and famous and are seen everywhere on TV and in the media. True greatness is built one brick at a time, one day at a time, stacking one daily habit on top of other, or repeating and reinforcing good habits until they are fully ingrained in our being and become unconscious reflex response .

Greatness is rooted in patience, effort, caring, loving, determination, helping, compassion, kindness, consistency, hard work and self-awareness. Anyone can be great at something. Greatness is quietly strong, it is deceptively quiet, and it is those who have qualities of discipline, love, compassion, and strong character that have achieved the most prolific heights of achievement. It is not necessary to be loud, gregarious, and aggressive or Type A personality to be a champion or achiever. History is filled with people who have had a quiet presence leading to legendary status. If you choose to display these qualities on a daily basis, you are a champion, simple as that. Keep doing that over years and years until you see the direct results these magical qualities yield, then you will be convinced.

Yes it may go unnoticed and unrecognized; you may not organize a Million Man March or win the Masters but it will not go unnoticed to YOU and that is what counts. You may not be getting the Super Bowl MVP award in front of millions of people but you are acting and establishing behavioral patterns matching the greats, which makes you great. They may get the Super Bowl ring but you get the "mom/dad of the year award", you get the "best spouse" award, you could get the "community leader" of the year award, you're crowned the "most influential", "best neighbor"; whate er it is.

In addition to all great things that you don't know are coming your way, you get to feel great and be strong, you get to be a beast and at the top of your game of life, with swagger and confidence all while wearing a big smile. You get to be healthy, happy, vibrant, fit, strong, sharp, joyful and loving. This is the life of a champion. It isn't that hard to achieve; you simply need to establish solid daily habits surrounding the "new you" and be militant in your discipline to who this person is.

Do not let yourself down: *this is all about not letting yourself down.* Whatever you have chosen to do, it is now 100% about not letting yourself down. If you tell yourself you are going to do something and don't do it, you have lied to yourself and this is a momentum killer. This is the kiss of death. The momentum is exactly what you need to use to gather speed to reach desires. To reach your goals you need all of the help possible along with some luck and the forces that reside inside you. Reaching goals is difficult. The attainment of them requires that all forces are working in your favor and in synchronicity.

"Whatever you have chosen to do, it is now 100% about not letting yourself down"

The most useful forces that are in your corner and available to you are: willpower, mental toughness, desire, momentum, character, discipline and staying power. As the universe operates in perfect fl w with all forces, make sure you make proper use of your given forces. Treasure these forces as your friend and best assets; they will be your guide in times of weakness. They will not steer you wrong, you can always count on your willpower, resilience, character and the universal fl ws that are on your side. They will never let you down. Don't go with the fl w, be the fl w.

The problem when you let yourself down is that, if you do it enough, it gets easier to quit. Do not let yourself down and you won't quit; it's that simple. Make a fi m commitment to yourself and keep it; this is the required mindset of master achievement. If you make a plan, stick to it no matter what: no excuses. What is required now is constant reinforcement of positive thought behaviors towards your desire. Ask yourself, "do I have the desire to rise above who I am and what I have right now?" Ask yourself if you are happy where you are in life, ask yourself if you are happy with who you are, ask yourself how it looks 2 years from now if you put in the work, ask yourself how much you care about your life and how it will turn out.

"The problem when you let yourself down is that, if you do it enough, it gets easier to quit"

Start living the life of a warrior and develop the qualities of a champion; your stock will rise. Your outside world reflects your inside world. Everything is there for the taking and available to anyone who has the desire and is willing and determined to assert enough of their willpower to make it happen.

"Not following through on what you told yourself is a deathwish to achievement"

Keeping commitments that you make to yourself is by far the most critical characteristic of high achievers. They will very rarely not do the things that they told themselves they would do. You really need to come to terms with this if you want to achieve more in your life. There needs to be a steadfastness and a resolve about you that won't permit quitting because it's not going your way. Make a plan, create the daily habits around the plan and under no circumstances let yourself down by not showing up and executing your plan. Not following through on what you told yourself is a death wish to achievement. Not completing the commitment you made to yourself will immediately fill you with sorrow, perhaps guilty feelings and certainly displeasure, which will knock you off course taking you further away from your desires. Not following through on your personal commitments to yourself leads to regret and disappointment. These are two of the most powerfully weakening qualities in human beings. Champions do exactly what they say they will do. They stay the course because they know how important that momentum is as they execute their thoughts and plans.

People who achieve always have the answer to why they are doing what they are doing. If it is a peaceful mind that you are mastering, you will know that you are meditating to quiet your mind and create peace within. If getting up at 5 am and going to the gym is your deal, you'll know your "why", so you can get in better shape and maybe meet someone who is also fit and healthy, or it could be so that you can be healthier and stronger for longevity in life, or it could be so you become disciplined in your daily habits. Whatever the reason you must be deeply committed to the "why" or the reason you desire it.

Master achievers get up early. People who get up early learn to get up early, they teach themselves. They start on day 1 and continue until it becomes a daily habit that they cannot live without. When you choose to change your habits, this is what will happen to you. You will start on day 1 and it will be a struggle for a little bit; this is natural and to be expected.

People who wake up early tend to eat breakfast, while later risers are often rushing out the door and have to grab something convenient (i.e. unhealthy), or they skip the meal altogether. If you're hungry because you missed a meal, the doughnut in the break room may be too tempting to resist. Similar to the breakfast example above, people who get up later in the day tend to focus less on healthy morning habits like hydrating and exercise, which oxygenates your blood and promotes overall health. People who wake up early also tend to have regular sleeping habits, unlike the night owls who keep erratic sleeping schedules.

When you exercise in the morning, you're less likely to have an excuse. Plus, you'll find that your morning workout will keep you energized all day long; this is contrary to what most people think. There is a tendency to believe that, if you workout in the morning, you will be tired all day. This may be the case for the first little while of your new workout schedule but, after 30 days, the early morning exercise will invigorate you all day.

"When you exercise in the morning, you're less likely to have an excuse"

Starting your day early improves your concentration. In addition to being able to focus on goals and task lists without being interrupted by family members or coworkers, getting up early means that by the time you get to work or school, you've had hours to properly acclimate yourself to the day. You'll be more alert during peak hours as a result.

Most successful people report that they're up at 5 am, or even earlier. Early risers tend to be more productive for a variety of reasons, including having more time to focus on important tasks while the rest of the world is asleep. This also translates to fewer interruptions. Brains tend to be most alert in the morning. If you're able to focus without interruptions early in the day, you'll get more done. You tend to make better decisions and think more clearly in the morning than in the afternoon and evening. Setting your goals first thing will help you achieve them. If you can manage to get out of bed early, you'll find that you have more energy throughout the day. It seems counterintuitive, but there are countless testimonials.

One of the most magical times of the day for the early riser is getting into nature before the world wakes up. We have all been there and know how magical this time of day can be for our spirt and our soul. Your job now is to have nature be part of your everyday activity, to be part of your daily routine. Whatever you are building for yourself, part of it should be nature regularly.

Can you imagine for a minute the cumulative effect that getting 30 minutes in nature will have on your soul after a few months? It is an unequivocal fact that we gather strength in nature, we recharge best in nature and nature is good for our souls, especially if you are near a body of water as the negative ions from the water have been proven to strengthen our state of mind.

Nature is pure effortless perfection. Nature contains the laws of the universe and it makes us feel good when we are close to this universal creation and fl w. Getting into nature in the early morning awakens our inner spirt and allows our soul's centre to lift and calibrate properly. Otherwise, you run the risk of carrying forward the negative emotions or feelings from yesterday. Getting into nature provides a clean slate for your day. It affords you the opportunity to sit peacefully with your own mind and create your own world. Get into nature; it may well be one of the best things you do.

"Nature is pure effortless perfection"

Keeping your body on a sleep routine will make it easier to go to sleep at night and to wake up naturally at the same time each morning. This is important for your body's internal clock. If you go to bed late and wake up late on the weekends it's harder for your body to adjust. People who get up early are naturally sleepier when it's the "normal" time to go to bed. Being on a predictable routine will help you sleep better each night and awaken feeling more rested. Sometimes it amazes me that not everyone gets up earlier. It's a miracle how quiet the world is first thing in the mo ning.

Getting up early is difficult for lots of people. For those of you who struggle, here are a few suggestions to rise early and enjoy the magic of the early morning. If you typically wake up at 8 am and decide that tomorrow you want to be out of bed by 5 am, you're setting yourself up for failure. Instead, try waking up just 15 minutes earlier each day. Within a week, you'll have worked your way up to almost two hours. If a week is too short of a time frame to make this adjustment, then space it out over two weeks or a month, but not longer than that.

Start going to bed earlier than you normally would, that way you'll get enough hours of sleep, and you won't feel deprived when the alarm goes off. If you're not tired when it's time to catch some Z's, then read a couple pages of a book, especially a boring one, and you'll be in dreamland in no time. Unless you naturally wake up at your goal time every morning, you're going to need to set an alarm. I recommend putting it across the room so you have to get out of bed to turn it off. I set the alarm to play an inspirational or energetic song to help nudge me out of bed. Something with a positive message

or an upbeat sound is much better to wake up to than a series of obnoxious beeps. Put the alarm clock outside of your
bedroom; put enough distance between you and that
blissful amazing mattress.

You need to have a good reason to get up early. And no,
your long list of emergencies is not the driver that should
spring you out of bed every morning. Instead, think of something positive that you plan on accomplishing. Maybe you can
tell yourself something like you'll get to leave work early if you
arrive earlier. If you enjoy meditating but don't often have the
time, use that as a reason to get up and start your day. Or you
can get a 45 minute workout in or do some journaling. Is there
a book you've wanted to read or an online class you've been
considering enrolling in? An extra skill set that would help
boost your career? Use the extra time you get in the morning
to do something that helps you grow and improve. By rising
early, you're rewarding yourself. Try to remember that.

"The medical community generally agrees that the best time to wake up is at sunrise"

Even though eating before bed can make you sleepy, it's
also been known to disrupt your sleep. If your tummy is grum-
bling, try a soothing cup o herbal tea instead o a carb filled
snack. Even if you tell yourself the night before that you plan
on rising before dawn, it's almost like you have a second personality that takes over when the alarm goes off and urges you
to go back to sleep; it's unnerving. To avoid that evil monster
living inside your brain, you're going to have to be firm. I you
can't reason with it, then you'll need to set up external cues in
your environment. I recommend putting a reminder on your
phone about your commitment or repeating the mantra "I de-

serve to be happy, inspired and full of enthusiasm when I wake because I am really looking forward to what and who I am in 6 months."

What is the best time to wake up? The answer to this question will vary depending on whom you ask. A lot of CEOs and gurus will tell you 5 am. However, the medical community generally agrees that the best time to wake up is at sunrise. The most important thing to keep in mind is consistency. Set a time that you plan to wake up at and stick to it.

What's the importance of a morning routine? A morning routine sets the tone for your entire day. This is especially true if you're forcing yourself to get up early and you're not naturally an early riser. Having a set routine each morning will help you stay focused and productive. Countless productivity experts agree that the first thing you do in the morning is to make your bed. It gives you a small win and you can claim completing that task as your first accomplishment of the day! By now you should be convinced that there are countless benefits to getting up early and no negatives. Try it for a week and see what kind of a difference it makes in your attitude, energy levels, and productivity.

Achievement thrills with a sense of newness that inspires creativity and excitement. When master achievers reach one level of success, they are immediately curious about what could be next. They begin charting innovative paths to get to something even larger. They feed their hunger one achievement at a time to live a life of success, happiness and satisfaction. They build one brick at a time as they know this is the only way. Master achievers perceive themselves as elite in their field; they never wallow in feelings of inferiority. By learning to climb the ladder of success, they overcome uncertainty and come out victorious. They accept that uncertainties and insecurities will come along the way but they use the challenge as fuel.

Master achievers do not see limits, they see possibilities. Exceptionally successful people neither run from nor dwell on their fears. They confront the fears most people shy away from. They recognize fear and doubt as the two biggest enemies to their success. Fear and doubt are all mental. High achievers feel these emotions, just as anyone else, but make the required effort not to be influenced by them. The successful elite use mental discipline and hard work to cultivate the habits that override these two negative counter forces.

The mark of a courageous person is the willingness to face what they fear. Master achievers habitually do the very things that scare them as a systematic desensitization process that build up their resilience and mental toughness. The more they expose themselves to fearful situations, the less power fear has over them. A person with the ambition to reach the top of their field must confront the fears holding them back. That is what makes someone powerful and allows them to push through the parts where weakness enters their mind. Weakness enters their minds just like yours except they don't let it paralyze or stop them from what they want. It becomes their thermometer as to whether or not the task is large enough. If they are not afraid, the challenge isn't big enough.

"The mark of a courageous person is the willingness to face what they fear"

People who achieve live with an unwavering commitment. They live with an intense belief in themselves, their business, their purpose and mission. They believe in the services they sell and in the quality of their customers. This deep belief cuts through the uncertainty and wavering that a less committed person would trip over on their path to success. High achievers know there is a one-to-one relationship between the depth of their belief and what happens in their reality.

They believe wholeheartedly in the rightness and goodness of what they stand for, what they are trying to achieve and what it will take to achieve it. This deep belief is the catalyst for creating their phenomenal reality. Those who are not committed tend to live emptier lives. Master achievers know that caring deeply is a critical element in life. All people who enjoy great lives care deeply about what they do and the people with whom they do it.

"A person who has prepared thoroughly has no fear or doubt when presenting ideas or when deciding on new opportunities"

Master achievers are always prepared. Truly successful people do not procrastinate; research and preparation keep them ahead of the game. They do the things the average person is unwilling to do. They make the necessary sacrifices to keep pace with the elite-of-the-elite. That is what makes them extraordinary. A master achiever never goes into a meeting unprepared. They do the research necessary to get themselves and their team to the next level of advancement. They do not leap at every deal that comes their way. They thoroughly review every detail of a new deal or collaboration before deciding whether to take it on. Preparation is the foundation of confidence. A person who has prepared thoroughly has no fear or doubt when presenting ideas or when deciding on new opportunities. Being prepared and informed is what makes master achievers smart decision-makers and great leaders.

Master achievers are passionate about learning. The excitement of not knowing fuels their curiosity and motivates them to take their new ideas to the next level. There is no room for ego or complacency in the lives of master achievers. They are always open to learning and never assume they know it all because that would limit their creativity and leave no room for more success.

"They thoroughly review every detail of a new deal or collaboration before deciding whether to take it on"

These types of people are in continual self-development. They tend to be avid journal writers, involved in professional development groups, training and seminars. They voraciously read whatever they can get their hands on to become bigger, wiser, happier and more satisfied in life and career. Those who are in-it-to-win-it live the belief that, if they are not working to get better, they are getting worse. Standing still in life is like being on a slow moving treadmill, you have to keep moving forward slowly just to stay even, move faster to get ahead; if you stop moving, you will fall off the back of the treadmill.

People who are wise in the areas of self-awareness and self-management are the greatest successes. These types of people are fiercely accountable. They know their biggest management challenge is managing themselves. They do not view themselves as working for someone else, even if they do. They are "self" employed in the sense that they know to get to the top of their field they have to be accountable for getting themselves there. They see themselves as the one constant they can influenc , control and change. Master achievers take full responsibility for who they are and never put blame on others for their failures. They examine what failed, look for what they can improve and make immediate efforts to do that. They view themselves as owning their careers, lives, finance , family, choices and relationships. They take complete responsibility.

"The super successful have learned that success is a process, not an event"

The successful elite use all challenges to fuel their creativity and their drive toward more success; letdowns are viewed as painful learning opportunities for greater advancement. The super successful have learned that success is a process, not an event. They expect to have good and bad days, experiences, deals and failures. All experiences, good and bad, are used for their promotion, personal transformation and education. Hindsight provides them with the understanding and gratitude for why it all had to happen the way it did. Master achievers know success in life and career results from using each challenge along the road to their benefit

TAKEAWAYS

- People who do remarkable or even great things are just normal people who worked hard for a long time. You have been given everything that anyone else has been given and in most cases you have been given more than most. You're just carrying around baggage or your stories from your past, master achievers aren't. They have freed themselves of their past.

- Your past is like everyone else's past; it has been difficult, you have lost love, lost friends, lost a spouse, someone sued you, had no money, lost a job, whatever your suffering entails. Welcome to Club Life, that's all of us. Grieve but get over it and move on.

- To have any chance at achieving at a high level, you must rid yourself of your past.

- Achievement is grounded in curiosity excitement, determination and consistency.

- Don't think that achievement only revolves around money. Realize money is a part of it but far from its core. You can achieve at almost anything. People achieve at all sorts of stuff: farming, painting, exercise, linguistics, dog training, food, etc. It's not all about the money. Know the "why" behind what

- you are doing; it will keep you going during the hard times.

- Don't let yourself down. This is 100% about not lying to yourself, be true to your mission. Not following through on what you committed to is a deathwish to achievement.

- Achievement is a process. All people who have achieved anything followed a process and proven rituals. Achievement is not a mystery; it is available to anyone; all you need is some desire and passion for something.

- Most successful people report they are up at 5am. Early morning rising is very good for your soul. Become involved with nature in some form.

CHAPTER 10

HOME FREE

There are not many feelings that beat the feeling of being certain to succeed at something because you have done the most difficult part. As you finish this book, you have put in some hard work. You have gone inside, you analyzed your perceptions, you questioned your beliefs, you understand yourself and people much better, you executed forgiveness, quieted your mind, gotten out of your comfort zone, matched your daily habits with your desires, strengthened your spirit and grown from your losses and failures. You have truly traveled within.

Now there is nothing that can stop you **except you**. This is the way of the enlightened and powerful; this is arriving at the middle ground. You no longer live at the extreme edges of life where your energy is vacuumed from you. Your energy is now intentional and dispersed for your own good. You have always had this energy; now, you have accessed it. Not only is this heightened energy at the ready, it is a powerful energy that can be stored inside and harnessed at will. You now have an endless reserve of patience, understanding, calmness, gratitude and strength.

Powerful emotions like kindness, unity, love, compassion, discipline and forgiveness, will be at your beck and call for the rest of your days. This is heightened understanding and deepened living. The world is no longer yours to take on, no longer yours to fix and has become a place of solace, wonder and amazement. Everything that transpires in front of you now is amazing and your curiosity will naturally manifest when you see the world as you see it now. A more childlike version of you will emerge, always asking questions, searching to understand other people, laughing, smiling and playing around. Now you say what you feel, laugh like you've always wanted, tell people about the real you, no longer apologizing, revealing yourself to the world, being excited about the real you.

"A more childlike version of you will emerge"

The real you is the only you that will ever walk the face of the earth in billions of years. Always keep in mind that you came from a sperm that can't be seen unless under a microscope. You came from nothing and end up as nothing. Be fantastically amazed at yourself, you'll be the only one like you EVER; isn't that amazing enough? While you are here on Earth, please allow yourself to come out and be seen. You will be amazed at how much we all love you. You will be amazed at how much you can love yourself. There is great power in this. Remove the mask and enjoy the beauty as it unfolds directly in front of you in ways you never thought possible. Release your vulnerabilities and your insecurities which will ultimately release you.

The events in life that don't make sense are now simply OK not to make sense. Everything doesn't have to make sense all of the time. The number one skill of the enlightened is they are able to let things be the way they are without pushing away or pulling towards

Our minds have been leading us astray since the beginning. As mentioned in Chapter 3, Raising Happy Adults, this stunted growth process starts at a very early age through our upbringing and into the formative school years. As we evolve and interact with those around us we begin to develop our perceptions and paradigms. Our minds start to become conditioned by our environmental upbringing. As a result, our minds begin thinking the only way it knows how. As well as our brains functions and keeps us alive, in the end, it starts to give us wrong responses, getting us into the wrong relationships, telling us we are afraid when we are not, making us believe things that aren't true.

How many times have you said something that you wish you could take back? How many times have you overreacted, responded poorly, lied to someone, done something you should not have done, surprised yourself with your behaviour or said something you should not have said? These are all acts of the mind. You sincerely thought at the time that the behaviour or decision was the best one to make but in hindsight, it was not the best decision. This means your mind gave you inaccurate or paradigmatic thoughts on which to react.

"If you tell yourself you are going to do something and don't do it (because you didn't feel like it) you have lied to yourself"

People lie to themselves fairly regularly. People even put the lies that they lie to themselves about into the world thinking it is a solution. If you tell someone you are going to help them move their apartment on Saturday and don't show up because you didn't feel like it, you have lied to that person. There are millions of examples of lying. If you tell yourself you are going to do something and don't do it (because you didn't feel like it) you have lied to yourself. If you tell yourself that you are going to get up at 5am to exercise and get into nature and you wake up at 7:30 am with just enough time to rush to work, you have lied to yourself. If you said that you aren't going to drink alcohol during the week and you have a couple of glasses of wine on Wednesday, you have lied to yourself. How many times have you told yourself that you were going to start something and simply didn't or started and had it fizzle out in short order?

You can try and sugar coat it all you want but it remains what it is. A lie is a lie whether it is to you or to someone else. People have just become very good at justifying the lies to themselves somehow finding a way to be OK with their perfidious mind. <u>Don't let yourself down</u>. This single principle has an enormous compounding effect.

Our minds trick us by telling us the wrong information fairly regularly. You will tell yourself that you can't do something because you are afraid. Think about it, how many times you have wanted to do something and your mind said that you were afraid to do it, and as a result you didn't do it? How many times has your caution and fear stopped you in your tracks when you were excited to do something? How many times have you thought you had a great idea only to have it shot down by a family member or friend, quashing it forever?

A moment of inspiration, a thought of brilliance, a thought of a greatness there one moment and gone the next, up in smoke. And where did this fear come from? Your mind. You fabricated it, made it up, gave it life and let it sit like an anchor in your mind. Your mind has tricked you to believe it's keeping you safe. This is far from the truth. The mind is doing you a disservice and handicapping you by telling you this. It is stopping you from the very thing that you should be doing which is acting on your insecurities and your fears, tackling them head-on causing them to leave you forever.

"Your mind has tricked you to believe it's keeping you safe"

At the beginning of time, safety was mandatory otherwise we would have died from natural forces of the universe, storms, dinosaurs, big animals; we lived in caves. Our minds at that time were a perfect fit for the environment; not so much today. When there is no fear we make it up, when there are no problems we create them, when we have moments of inspiration the mind quashes them with excuses. The mind will tell you something that you want to do is too hard. It will tell you that you are too tired, making you quit; it will defeat you before you even start.

Your mind has a bank account of memorized stories and feelings purely designed to keep you safe. You can regurgitate and retell these stories and express these emotions at will. These are the stories that protect your insecurities from ever being exposed or revealed. You have created all sorts of stories about yourself that you simply made up so your resolve is never tested. These stories insulate your fears from coming under attack. These stories and feelings will hold you back if they don't disappear from your mind. You made them up so you can unmake them. Yes, it's that simple. If you tell yourself they are gone, they are gone. Your mind plays tricks on you; don't worry, it happens to everyone. Do not trust your mind and you misguided thoughts, trust your soul. Your soul not only knows the truth and the truth has no way of acting outside of it.

"These are the stories that protect your insecurities from ever being exposed or revealed"

Your mind will tell you that you shouldn't ask that girl out because of how you might feel about her reply. Your mind will prevent you from taking on challenges that you really want to do, it will tell you that your marriage will get better, "I just have to give it more time". It will tell you that you don't have enough money, that you aren't pretty enough, athletic enough, too short, too tall, too fat, too skinny, not enough muscles, your head is too big, too white, bad haircut, too poor, can't be that rich, it even tells you that it is OK to spend time in a negative environment with people you know aren't good for you. I don't know how and why we think this way but it is time to let your soul take the wheel and bring a little more balanced perspective and approach to your life. Allow your new found enlightenment to guide you.

We can trust our soul unequivocally because this is where you live and it is here that knows the truth. Your soul cannot lie to itself, it doesn't have this ability. Listen to the soul's guidance not the guidance of the meandering and drifting mind. The soul is the place where you and all of your wonderful characteristics live that help you create your life. You can always trust your soul in times of difficulty or turmoil. Using your soul to guide you will bring any difficulty to its knees swiftly because the soul has no fear, it knows only the truth. It is the mind that makes up the fear and non-truth. Don't let your mind run wild, do not resist events that should not be resisted. The universe only wants to give and not take.

What would happen if you started to look at life a little bit different from the way you do? Suppose you knew that what had happened in your life, which you termed a loss or failure, was exactly what was supposed to happen? Suppose you knew immediately that you *had to* experience the event that triggered your pain and struggle? Then suppose you could chose to act in accordance with this new awareness. Often is the case that we think something is causing us sorrow or grief at the time but actually it turns out to be the foundational requirement of something much better that is about to occur in the future. Almost like it was supposed to be this way the whole time. You know the times, when you lost the girlfriend or boyfriend and were devastated, then 2 months later you were dating someone way better. The time you got fired from your job and were devastated only to have a way better job show up months later. The time you left your spouse and were devastated only to end up in the arms of love.

If we could just change our perception in these moments it can change your life. Undoubtedly this "supposing" conflicts with all that you have been taught about how you're supposed to react in catastrophe or struggle. I am not suggesting you not respect your genuine feelings, rather I am suggesting this perspective offers you another way of responding to these kinds of circumstances. I am encouraging you to open the gift or value that is also found in sorrow.

There will always be steps backwards, the key is not to make them repeatedly. Don't even take two steps backwards, take one step and stop. This is the absolute key to stopping the downward spiral and keeping you in harmony. The moment the initial thoughts of resistance comes in, and yes they will still come in regularly, the energy and thoughts you put towards it must be stopped. Realize the valley is only a few more bad decisions away. The ditch is only a couple more steps backwards. We all know how difficult it is to lift ourselves out of the valley or out of a very difficult time that you've been through. Once we have suffered and reached a low point in our lives, it can be quite a struggle to get out from under the emotional pain.

The reason that it is so hard to get out of a valley is that all of our prime mental resources become deployed to fix the problem leaving us no energy for growth. Every thought in every waking hour is spent trying to shore up the problem, trying to make sense of it and trying to create the solution to get out from under it. We now must spend all of our energy on this problem until it is fi ed. We send all of our emotions and thoughts in the direction that is opposite to where we are going. We need to avoid these extremes. The extremes are very time consuming and only serve to push us further away from the very thing we want.

If you want to know why these thoughts are running around madly in your head in the first place, don't do them. If you are balding and have insecurity around this resulting in you wearing a hat, don't wear the hat and it will reveal your insecurity and the reasons behind your insecurity. Without knowing why you are insecure or fear something, you will never unearth why it is stopping you from being you. If you want to know why you are afraid to speak in front of a group, go speak in front of a group, it is a surefire ay to expose you to yourself.

If your insecurity forces you to wear baggy clothes to hide all signs of your extra weight, walk around in more revealing clothes and you will soon see why you are insecure about your weight. You will soon see that it has nothing to do with your clothes, your follicle challenge, your car, your house, your family or anything else. You will soon begin to understand how the model you built in your mind is fractured.

No one cares about your hair, your weight, your car or

really anything else for that matter. You are telling yourself what you need to tell yourself so that you can avoid what you need to do to change your mindset and state of being. Realize that the model you have built for yourself is a house of cards. You must allow your new found enlightenment to open the portal to your authenticity.

Once you are able to be still in the now, the weight of the world will be lifted. There is absolutely no reason for anyone to carry any weight of this world or any other world, why would there be? When we are born, we are given a name, given some clothes and, if we are lucky, had some people around to help raise us. We are told how to behave, we watch our parents behave, we are sponges soaking up everything that comes our way from those around us. This is just how it goes for all of us. How you were raised and what you learned is not who you are. It just is what it is. Good or bad, these are the people you have been around and learned from; we all have them. Enlightenment is when you realize you are not your past, your name, your body or your thoughts but the soul or consciousness behind it all.

"Once you are able to be still in the now, the weight of the world will be lifted"

The moment this realization washes over you is the moment you are home-free. This is the moment when your problems now become opportunities and your defeats become victories. A certain clarity rises to the surface of your mind. This is the moment your thoughts, perceptions and your entire existence does a U-turn lifting you to spirited optimism. Living with contentment, peace, happiness, strength and ease are all hallmarks of enlightenment. You will begin to see people the way they are, *which is exactly like you.*

You will quite naturally and easily become curious about other people. Be true to this curiosity and watch life's multiplication unfold before you. Watch the waves that occur from dropping this rock of excitement into the water. You will begin to act in harmony with the universe and with yourself. You will no longer be lying to yourself as it has become obvious how self-defeating this is for your spirit. There will be a cleansing of your soul, your past will melt away and be completely irrelevant.

> *"This is the moment your thoughts, perceptions and your entire existence does a U-turn lifting you to spirited optimism"*

Your will look to the future with anticipation, as a source of inspiration and joy; something worth looking forward to. You will begin to wonder how in the world you wasted so much of your life wandering around thinking about all the nonsense that you did, behaving how you did and acting the way you used to. You'll be left wondering how a particular co-worker from the office ever took a single thought of your time let alone the months of which you were robbed.

You now have a clean slate; isn't that exactly what you've been waiting for? The ability to wash away your past and create the future that you so passionately believe in. Just listen carefully and objectively to your thoughts; no need to act on any of them if you don't want to. Allow your judgements of people and perceptions of situations to take your attention only briefly and then let them pass through you, only giving your energy to the thoughts that are inspiring or uplifting. Act on the thoughts surrounding opportunity, creation, love, helping, giving, building, and joining. This is how perception is meant to work. It is meant to take things in, and let them pass through you so that you can be fully present in the next moment. This is what it is meant to be alive, having experiences that pass through you, awaken you and stimulate you. Moment after moment, experience after experience, you are now learning and growing. When we live in this state we are a fully aware being.

Nobody is making this stuff up, it is real, and it works. It has been here a long time before you showed up and will be here a long time after you leave. These principles are the results of the culmination of the world's existence and ancient human history. These principles are very effective and yield immediate and profound results. It is really just up to you if you choose to implement them. The universe doesn't care what you do, other people don't care what you do, but you should!!

"Nobody is making this stuff up, it is real, and it works"

Now that you understand yourself you can truly begin to understand other people. This is a very valuable asset. Being curious and wondering about people is a gift that yields many rewards. The biggest reward in this process is that you will develop very deep relationships with other people. This is only because you have taken the time to understand yourself. If you understand yourself, you will most certainly understand your partner(s). Understanding yourself keeps the curiosity in you alive, asking questions until you deeply understand the people in your relationships.

You no longer have such high stakes in how you fit in the equation. Your focus on you will slowly fade and your relationships will begin to be much more about the other person. How can I help them, it seems like they are having a tough time, what can I do to help? I didn't realize that she loved going on walks so much; let's make sure we go for a walk once a week. I see his car is a bit messy, maybe I'll have it detailed for him as a surprise. This is where your world wakes up. A new vibrancy or frequency calibrates within you. This is the enlightenment frequency, the frequency of the middle ground. These are the vibrations, energy levels or states of being that you must use to your advantage. These "good vibes" only know attraction along with multiplication and act in great synchronicity with universal fl ws.

"You no longer have such high stakes in how you fit in the equation"

You can physically feel people with good vibrations when you see them. Being on this vibration frequency only serves you for your good. This is the fantastic state of attraction. You see, people love being around other people who are on this frequency. Why? Because everyone wants to be on this frequency. This is pure gold. When people see others whose frequency is higher than theirs, they simply want to stop what they are doing and somehow talk or be with that person so the vibrational frequency can rub off on them. Everyone wants this frequency and we will do what we can to get it.

What you realize now is that you have a tremendous amount of energy inside you. You have enough energy inside you to light up a city. This energy is available to you whenever you want and for whatever reason you want to use it. You know the feeling when you are full of energy, you feel like you could take on the world. The only reason you don't feel this energy all the time is that you block it. You block it by allowing thoughts into your psyche and into your heart, by closing your mind, and pulling yourself into the restrictive space inside. This immediately closes off your energy supply. What you end up doing is hiding in the darkness inside of you. This is what it means to be disturbed or blocked. This is the exact reason why you have no energy when you are depressed.

"Lighten up, the lighter you take yourself and the more you detach from self-importance, the more you will attract in your life"

Remember that your field of energy radiates at whatever vibratory frequency you generate. You are impacting and being impacted by the energy fields of other people every day. Don't give your energy to situations or people that you don't want or believe in. Anytime you opt for anger rather than laughter, fasting rather than feasting, suffering rather than pleasure or grieving rather than celebrating, you are making a choice to slow down your vibrations and to pollute your immediate mental energy field. Lighten up, the lighter you take yourself and the more you detach from self-importance, the more you will attract in your life. We have complete control over the amount of laughing, singing and rejoicing we do. Regardless of how much we have convinced ourselves to the contrary.

How you choose to use your energy effects every part of your life. Where and how you choose to use your energy creates your feelings and your feelings create your existence. Ask yourself, am I happy, angry, anxious, relaxed, easy going, mean spirited, stressed out or happy-go-lucky? Whatever you are, look to where you are putting your thoughts and energy. How you feel emotionally is in direct proportion to what you choose to think about and subsequently put your energy towards. The only way to change how you feel is to change what you think about.

"Everyone is exactly where they are supposed to be at this exact time"

Thoughts and energy choices will give you whatever you request of them. Your energy can open up amazing relationships or it can close doors to them. The energy you send out into the world is directly related to where you are in your life. Everyone is exactly where they are supposed to be at this exact time despite protests from most that it is someone else's fault or it was an event that caused them to be where they are. Life is energy and you are energy within life.

The way you think has a ripple effect through your mind and body, a vibratory action. Don't use weakening energies employed by those around you. Other people can't bring you down if you are operating at the higher energies. Why? Because quicker and higher energies nullify and convert the slower/lower energies, not the opposite. When you feel like the lowered energies around you are pulling you down, it is only because you are deciding to join them at their lower energy levels. When you react to the lower energies you encounter with your own similar low energies, you are creating a scenario that attracts more of that negative energy.

It is clear that in removing lower energy obstacles, we must raise ourselves to the levels of energy where we *are* the happiness we desire, we *are* the love we feel is missing, we *are* the abundance we strive for. By being it, we attract it to us. By condemning its absence, we ensure the disharmony and discord continues to fl w in our lives. If you're experiencing lack, general unhappiness, suffering, affliction, or any inability to attract what you desire, seriously look at how you've been attracting these circumstances into your life. Low energy is an attractor pattern. It is there because you have summoned it, even if on a subconscious level. Once you raise your energy levels by being aware of your environment, you will begin to remove all of those self-imposed obstacles.

You need to pay special attention to your energy fl w. If you like good energy or vibes, just don't ever close. You must concentrate on staying open, if you can, the more energy will fl w into you. It is after receiving lots of energy that you will realize that all you have ever really wanted in this life is excitement, enthusiasm, happiness and love. If you can feel this way on the inside who cares what you're experiencing on the outside. If you can take this single step **you will get everything** that everyone else is struggling for. It is my hopes that you have now raised your energy level as a way to remove the obstacles that prevent you from experiencing the perfection that you are a part of.

Watch carefully now as you go through life experiencing the same things you experienced before just with this new lens. Feel your new perspective to these same events knowing confidently that you face them with a new set of skills. These are the moments you will feel the initial freedom from your mental cage. You will see that problems of old are opportunities of today. Casually notice people's attitude towards you change, observe when people look twice at you, feel the deeper more intentional eye contact, enjoy it when strangers begin to randomly talk to you, notice the unprovoked smiles from passersby, feel when you are happy doing nothing, revel in how the love you give brings back everything you ever desired. This is what it will feel like; these are the signs that you are enjoying the middle ground. Feel the love and warmth of all that is.

This is your gift now. With this gift comes much responsibility. You now have a responsibility to yourself and to others that you did not have before. In the past, you would let yourself or others down with no opposition from yourself. You had a pile of your excuses at the wait for anything that moved you out of your comfort zone. You were armed with the concocted stories about yourself only to insulate you from anything resembling discomfort. You were hijacked and didn't know it. Gone are all those stories you made up in your mind as excuses for when different events and levels of discomfort popped up. The old weapons of caution, hurriedness, agitation, stress, anxiety and fear have been traded in to give you the proper weapons for what lies ahead.

"As your spirit lifts and the chatter in your mind subsides, you have reached a heightened state of being"

Enlightened people carry weapons of kindness, curiosity, calm, resolve, strength, love, work, patience, understanding, discipline, peace, harmony, fl w, giving and acceptance for what is. These are the new tools of YOUR trade. These are the characteristics that are required to get to your next level. This is all you will ever need to get everything that you've ever desired. These qualities need to reside deep in your soul to be effective. Make sure these are burned into your being as non-negotiables and will not be dishonoured under any circumstance.

As your spirit lifts and the chatter in your mind subsides, you have reached a heightened state of being. As you move towards the middle ground, outward signs will begin to appear. More people will smile at you, you will receive more "good mornings" or "hellos" from strangers, people will stand closer to you, whether in a bank line up or at your local coffee shop, people will begin to ask you questions wanting to know more about you. You'll get more phone calls, more opportunities, more hugs, less stress, more happiness, more calmness, reduced anxiety and enjoy a significant increase in vitality and human wonderment. There are hundreds of tangible changes that occur, these are just a few.

"As you move towards enlightenment, outward signs will begin to appear"

Deep relationships are the key to the quality of this life. As you start anew, the quality of your relationships will increase significantl . New perspective brings with it new questions, new understanding, new magic. Just like a snake sheds its skin or a caterpillar emerges from the cocoon, they emerge renewed, reinvigorated and ready to create a new life. Here is your chance, exactly what you have been waiting for. An opportunity to finally be the person you have been creating and cajoling in your mind all these years. Enlightenment is an opportunity that only a select few receive because they have put in the work just like you have. With hard work comes rewards and your rewards are happiness, peace of mind, fulfillment, increased opportunity, powerful aura and all of the abundance this world has to offer. Enlightenment will not change your outer world but will change your way of processing the world.

Ask yourself, how much do I deserve to be happy and loving life? If you're after life's abundance, get started immediately and map out the plan that catapults you forward. Enlightenment is an inside job. Walking this path is a very personal experience and must be walked alone. Once you have walked the path, those who have gone before you will be right there waiting for your arrival. The middle ground is where there is no weakness, weakness cannot reside. What will come your way is exactly what you have been looking for all along. Great relationships with fantastic people, people who appreciate you, lift you, love you and help you reach heights you could not have reached on your own. Money will begin to fl w, fulfil - ment will increase as will your wonderment of this beautiful world we live in. This is exactly what you deserve, there will be no settling for second best when it comes to your life and the relationships in it.

Now that you have become acquainted with your "new self", you have discovered that you can approach infinite in- telligence, either for the purpose of offering thanks for what you already possess or to ask for more and for guidance. Fear is now replaced with faith and belief. This re-acquaintance with yourself will most certainly bring you closer to the understand- ing that nature and the universe work in perfect precision, as do you. The world revolves perfectly on an axis, the sun continues to send down its rays of warmth, causing the earth to yield an overabundance of food, water continues to fl w downhill, the stars shine nightly in their accustomed places, grass grows without effort, and fl wers bloom year after year.

Being home-free is being at ease with all that is, all that was and all that will be. Wherever you go, there you are. When you like you, others will like you as well. Being authentically you allows you to breathe easier experience less stress, making you more productive. This is the state of mind that will help you to change your material or financial status along with el- evating your levels of happiness and peace of mind. This is where you want your family- work relationship to be, fl wing and at ease. This is the lofty air that the 1% occupy and guess what, congratulations, you are now there amongst them in this rarified ai . It wasn't nearly as hard as you thought was it?

"You now reside in the hallowed grounds of enlightenment, authenticity and a oneness with the whole"

Now that you have accessed your quiet mind, you have arrived, the Holy Grail is yours; now things really start to happen. This is where your life will shift into the next gear without you even noticing, almost effortlessly. Look around and ask yourself how you got here? You now reside in the hallowed grounds of enlightenment, authenticity and a oneness with the whole.

This is where life begins and where no inventory is taken. This is the fertile grounds of growth, inspiration, change and renewal. As you inwardly surrender to the events that cause you resistance in life, no scars will form on your psyche. The impressions will only last while the event is taking place. Allow each event to shape you and reach you at a level where it forces you past foundational fears and boundaries. As long as you are prepared to accept the purification power of life's fl w, you will continually come out the other side as a more transformed person.

This is where your soul will remain completely undisturbed while you dance with life's universal fl ws. Allow the fl w of life to act like a washboard helping you to free yourself from you. At some point, there will be no more struggles, just a deep peace that comes from surrendering to a perfection that is beyond your comprehension. Eventually you will stop resisting and your heart will lose the tendency to close. Now that you are here, you will never turn back because the joy, happiness and peace are just too valuable to ever give up. Now that you are ready to let go of yourself, life will create doors where there were once windows. Life will truly become your friend.

"This is where your soul will remain completely undisturbed while you dance with life's universal flows"

You will recognize the fact that you have always been inside there, you have just been consumed and overwhelmed by the bombardment of thoughts and resistances that have been dwelling in your subconscious. This newfound quietness will soak into everything you do, your decision making, your choices, habits, behavioural patterns, verbiage and most importantly your heart. An open heart has lots of room for love and opportunity. An open heart by default and natural law, gravitates towards love.

With a quiet mind, your heart will have all of the room necessary to allow in the exact things you desire. Your desires cannot be realized if they are in opposition to the inner feelings of your heart and soul. Your thoughts, your words and your actions must be consistent with your desires. When you strive to achieve balance in your thoughts and actions, with living in the moment, you are now living in *harmony*.

To live in harmony with the world is enlightenment. You now are acting in accordance with the natural laws of the universe. Harmony is the ability to relate yourself to nature's laws, to have them help you, and the ability to relate yourself to other people to gain their harmonious, willing cooperation in helping you make life yield whatever you want from it. Time is nature's seasoning influence through which human experience may be ripened into a state of living in harmony. People are not born being in harmony. It takes many years, often decades, to gather the skills of acting in harmony with the universe. The good thing is people have the capacity to think and they may, through the lapse of time, think their way into a harmonious state of being.

Once you are harmonious within, your energy levels will increase automatically and you will be bringing higher vibrational energy to everyone you encounter. By doing this you will dissolve your own lower energies. When the energies of love, openness, compassion, creativity and abundance are present in your relationships you are enlightened. Now the forces begin to work on everyone and everything that is in your environment. The right person shows up, the new job appears, the funding is approved, and the phone rings with the good news you have been waiting for. Don't confuse these with coincidences, these are universal laws that fit perfectly together for your well being.

"To live in harmony with the world is enlightenment"

As we head home, it has become evidently clear why association with negative thoughts, people and actions are detrimental to self-determination and how absolutely critical your environment is to your well-being and happiness. Nature allows no one to escape their environment, it is simply how it operates; you become your environment.

As you sit in the seat of your soul and objectively observe your thoughts, the precious treasures of your time and energy will emerge to be used as fuel to power you to the top. Our journey together has given you access to one of life's greatest mysteries. You now have no choice but to take immediate account of your life and make the necessary modificati ns; to never look back. Your best self awaits.

It's all you now, enjoy the special place you are in. It only gets better from here. You are very well equipped to do this job. You have done the required inside work, you have examined yourself objectively, been able to see people and the world in a different light, you have maneuvered your perceptions for the better, you are able to blend into healthy and strong relationships, happiness is within you radiating from your soul, you are a distribution centre of love and peace, your soul has been released, you are forever free

"Being home-free is being at ease with all that is, all that was and all that will be"

TAKEAWAYS

- Create "you" in your mind, simply design the person you want to be and be that person. ALWAYS.

- If you have disturbances or blockages from the past, they MUST be removed at whatever cost.

- Create a "plan" to chase your desires. If you want stuff, you must have at least a decent plan.

- Create "daily habits" that nurture your desires and progress your plan.

- STAY TRUE to yourself and your daily habits: Don't let yourself down by being undisciplined and not carrying out your plan. If you start to let in a little water, over enough time the boat sinks. NO water gets in; be disciplined, stay the course. Don't lie to yourself!!

- Always be on guard for the unassuming **DOUBLE WORK LOAD** effect. If you take a day off when your plan doesn't allow for it, you have to work twice as hard and long to balance it out. Don't put that extra weight on yourself; right now is not the time for that.

- Don't let yourself down. Keep the commitments that you made to yourself.

- New perspective offers new life. Change your perceptions and change your life. What you think is terrible another sees as opportunity.

- How you choose to use your energy affects every part of your life, so choose wisely.

- Don't lie to yourself. The ensuing internal disappointment can be a momentum killer.

- With the disturbance and blockages removed, your heart now has room for the things you desire.

- Start immediately, stick to it and allow enough time to pass until the new habits become your lifestyle. Eventually you will not recognize the old you.

BRUCE ELLEMO

A speaker, entrepreneur, author, consultant, and coach, Bruce has transformed countless lives with his message of prosperity. For more than twenty five years Bruce has been motivating and helping people achieve success and abundance in both their personal and business lives. One of the best ways to cultivate the ability to ensure you are consistently locked into a positive, forward thinking and energetic mindset is to get help from others, people who have gone before us. The more we know the more context we have. The more complex our knowledge is, the better informed are our decisions.

If you're ready to level up and want to live your life by design without exceptions. Book a FREE strategy call with me personally!

During that short call we will sit down, design a plan that will get you or your business aligned with your vision and give you a plan of action you can move forward with starting today!

Visit this link to book a call now bruceellemo.net/work-with-me and discover what we have to offer.

We welcome the opportunity to serve you.

CONQUER FROM WITHIN

bruceellemo

RESOURCES FOR PERSONAL GREATNESS

BE Leadership International offers a complete range of learning tools and coaching services to help elevate you to your highest potential. To compete at a world class level you need the experience, enthusiastic support, objective perspective and the insight of a coach. This is just as true for CEO's, entrepreneurs, young graduates, business leaders and business professionals.

Imagine starting your day being coached by Bruce in a cutting edge format that develops you from the inside out ensuring your long term growth and success. A program that removes any doubt or insecurity and brings rise to your brilliance for you and the world to see. Sessions are offered in groups via Skype, one on one via skype or one on one in person. As you expand your awareness you expand your opportunities and unlock your highest potential. It's time to elevate your life, shed your fears, reconnect with your highest potential all while enjoying this life-changing system. Let's go on ths journey together.

The **Conquer From Within WEEKENDS** is a transformational experience that occurs three times per year over 2-3 days. All one on one clients are automatically included in this WEEKEND. You can also enroll in **The Exclusive Advanced Series** - a full year of personal development coaching with Bruce Ellemo. It will also be one of the funnest learning experiences you will have of the year. The Exclusive Advanced Series and Weekends change lives, period!!! For more details or to register for the next Weekend email admin@bruceellemo.com

Keynote Speeches and Leadership Seminars

Bruce is one of the most in-demand speakers and seminar leaders around today. His leadership concepts have helped many organizations rise above the competition. His presentations are deep,impactful, inspiring and full of modern world approach. He has shown employees in many organizations how to have tremendous work-life balance, resulting in a more impactful bottom line. For more on Bruce's presentations go to www.bruceellemo.com or email admin@bruceellemo.com